SOMATIC THERAPY SIMPLIFIED

EMPOWER YOUR MIND & BODY WITH EFFORTLESS HOLISTIC HEALING FOR MINDFULNESS, STRESS RELIEF, AND EMOTIONAL BALANCE

LINDA LEE SMITH

An LLS Digital Publishing Book/November 2024
All Rights Reserved
Copyright © 2024 Linda Lee Smith
Cover Design by *Pixel_Pulse*

The content within this book may not be reproduced, duplicated or transmitted without direct written permission from the author or the publisher.

Under no circumstances will any blame or legal responsibility be held against the publisher or author for any damages, reparation, or monetary loss due to the information contained within this book. Either directly or indirectly. You are responsible for your own choices, actions, and results.

Legal Notice:

This book is copyright-protected. This book is only for personal use. You cannot amend, distribute, sell, use, quote, or paraphrase any part of this book's content without the author's or publisher's consent.

Disclaimer

Please note the information contained within this document is for educational and entertainment purposes only. All effort has been expended to present accurate, up-to-date, reliable, and complete information. No warranties of any kind are declared or implied. Readers acknowledge that the author is not engaging in the rendering of legal, financial, medical, or professional advice. The content within this book has been derived from various sources. Please consult a licensed professional before attempting any techniques outlined in this book.

By reading this document, the reader agrees that under no circumstances is the author responsible for any losses, direct or indirect, which are incurred as a result of the use of the information contained within this document, including, but not limited to, — errors, omissions, or inaccuracies.

ISBN: 9798344349886

TABLE OF CONTENTS

Introduction	7
1. UNDERSTANDING SOMATIC THERAPY	11
What is Somatic Therapy?	12
The Science Behind the Mind-Body Connection	15
Key Principles of Somatic Therapy	18
How Somatic Therapy Complements Other Holistic Practices	21
Common Misconceptions About Somatic Therapy	23
2. GETTING STARTED WITH SOMATIC THERAPY	27
Preparing Your Mind and Body for Healing	28
Setting Intentions for Your Somatic Journey	31
Creating a Safe and Sacred Space for Practice	33
Tools and Resources to Support Your Practice	35
Establishing a Support Network	37
3. BODY AWARENESS TECHNIQUES	41
The Importance of Body Awareness	42
Simple Exercises to Enhance Body Awareness	44
Using Breathwork to Connect with Your Body	47
Guided Body Scanning Techniques	49
Developing a Daily Body Awareness Routine	51
4. RELEASING STORED TRAUMA	55
Understanding Trauma and Its Physical Manifestations	56
Self-Awareness and Mindfulness	58
Breathwork Techniques for Trauma Release	59
Therapeutic Movement for Emotional Release	61
Self-Massage Techniques for Trauma Release	64
Using Sound and Vibration to Aid Trauma Release	67
Using Self-Healing Techniques to Balance Your Energy	69
5. MANAGING STRESS AND ANXIETY	73
The Impact of Stress and Anxiety on the Body	74
Grounding Exercises for Instant Stress Relief	77

Mindfulness Practices to Reduce Anxiety	79
Creating a Stress-Relief Toolkit	81
Integrating Stress Management into Daily Life	84

6. ESTABLISHING SELF-CARE ROUTINES — 87
   - The Role of Self-Care in Somatic Therapy — 88
   - Designing a Personalized Self-Care Plan — 91
   - Creating a Morning Ritual to Balance Your Day — 92
   - Creating Evening Routines for Restorative Sleep — 95
   - Incorporating Nature into Your Self-Care Routine — 98

7. ENHANCING EMOTIONAL RESILIENCE — 103
   - Understanding Emotional Resilience — 104
   - Techniques to Strengthen Emotional Resilience — 107
   - Managing Overwhelming Emotions — 109
   - The Healing Power of Journaling — 111
   - Developing a Resilience-Building Routine — 114

8. INTEGRATING SOMATIC PRACTICES INTO DAILY LIFE — 117
   - Mindful Eating and Somatic Awareness — 118
   - Using Somatic Techniques at Work — 120
   - Incorporating Somatic Practices into Exercise — 122
   - Applying Somatic Principles to Relationships — 124
   - Making Somatic Practices a Lifelong Habit — 126

9. BUILDING A SUPPORTIVE COMMUNITY — 129
   - The Importance of Community in Healing — 130
   - Finding or Creating a Local Support Group — 133
   - Online Communities and Resources — 135
   - Sharing Your Somatic Journey with Others — 137
   - Fostering Connection and Empathy in Your Community — 139

10. TRACKING PROGRESS AND STAYING MOTIVATED — 143
    - The Importance of Tracking Your Progress — 144
    - Using Worksheets and Tools for Self-Assessment — 147
    - Staying Motivated and Overcoming Obstacles — 150

In Conclusion — 155
References — 159

I dedicate this book to all those ready to awaken awareness of their body/mind connection and willing to step out of the paradigms that hold them hostage to the past.

INTRODUCTION

I was on a Zoom call with a client a few years ago, listening to her struggles with stress and emotional imbalance. Ever since the COVID shutdown, she had retreated to her couch, playing the game of Solitude on her tablet. Life had grown stale, lonely, and uninteresting for her, a common thread during the shutdown. As she spoke, I could feel the weight of her worries and the toll it took on her body and spirit. She was reaching out to me for help. Then, I shared with her the transformative power of Somatic Therapy and life coaching, which helped her turn her life around over the next few months.

As a holistic nurse, coach, energy therapist, and aromatherapist, I can identify with the many positives of Somatic Therapy. This holistic approach connects the mind and body to promote healing and well-being. It integrates energy healing, aromatherapy, mindfulness, breath work, nature-based spirituality, therapeutic movement, journaling, and listening to inner wisdom. Somatic Therapy helps us achieve a harmonious balance by addressing physical and emotional aspects. Somatic Therapy is this great umbrella under which many holistic treatments find their niche.

The purpose of this book is to make Somatic Therapy simple and accessible. I want to guide you through various holistic healing practices I have come to love over the years that can help you find mindfulness, stress relief, emotional balance, and even relief of physical discomfort. My vision is to provide you with tools that are easy to follow and integrate into your daily life. Each chapter will offer practical techniques and insights to support your journey toward well-being, bringing you a sense of relief and comfort.

Holistic healing is significant because it acknowledges the interconnectedness of our mind, body, and spirit. When we address all these aspects together, we can experience profound and lasting healing. Many of us have spent years caring for others, often neglecting our own needs. This book invites you to prioritize your well-being and nurture yourself with compassion and care.

Somatic Therapy Simplified is written with you in mind, regardless of age or gender. It will help anyone seeking ways to overcome stress and emotional imbalance. Whether new to holistic practices or with some experience, it will offer valuable insights and techniques to support your journey. It is also for those across the age spectrum who are curious about exploring new ways to enhance their well-being. Everyone is welcome here.

The book's structure is designed to guide you through different aspects of Somatic Therapy. Each chapter focuses on a specific practice, starting with energy healing and moving through aromatherapy, mindfulness techniques, breath work, nature as a healer, therapeutic movement, journaling, and listening to inner guidance. By the end of the book, you will have a comprehensive toolkit to support your holistic healing journey.

Allow me to share a bit about myself. My name is Linda Lee Smith, and I am passionate about helping people achieve holistic well-being. I have spent years studying and practicing various healing modalities —Healing Touch, Reiki, aromatherapy, life coaching, and Transcendance™—and I have seen firsthand the transformative power of these practices. I aim to provide reputable, easy-to-follow guidance that anyone can use to enhance their well-being.

I invite you to join me on this journey of self-discovery and healing. As you read through this book, I encourage you to approach each practice with an open heart and mind. Take your time to explore and experiment with the techniques. Remember that healing is a personal and unique journey and finding what works best for you is essential. Rest assured, these techniques are effective and will guide you toward holistic healing.

Thank you for allowing me to be a part of your journey. I am honored to share these practices and support you in finding mindfulness, stress relief, and emotional balance. We can create a life filled with joy, peace, and well-being.

CHAPTER ONE

UNDERSTANDING SOMATIC THERAPY

A few years ago, I conversed with a woman I will call Emily. She had recently retired and was struggling with chronic back pain and relentless anxiety. Despite trying various medications and therapies, she felt trapped in a cycle of discomfort and stress. One day, after a particularly frustrating doctor's appointment, Emily decided to explore alternative healing methods on her own. This decision led her to Somatic Therapy, a choice that transformed her life. As she shared her experience with me, her eyes sparkled with relief and newfound hope. Emily's journey opened my eyes to the profound impact that Somatic Therapy can have on our lives, regardless of age who might be grappling with years of accumulated stress and trauma.

WHAT IS SOMATIC THERAPY?

Somatic Therapy is a holistic approach that integrates the mind and body to promote healing and well-being. It fundamentally focuses on the body and how emotions appear within it.

At its core, Somatic Therapy emphasizes body awareness, helping you tune into the physical sensations that often go unnoticed but hold the key to emotional and psychological healing. This form of therapy recognizes that our bodies store memories and emotions, manifesting as physical symptoms when left unaddressed. By focusing on these sensations, Somatic Therapy enables you to release stored trauma and stress, fostering a healthier, more balanced life.

According to an article in Harvard Health Publishing, Somatic Therapy may potentially help alleviate "Post-traumatic stress disorder (PTSD), complicated grief, depression, anxiety, trust and intimacy issues, and self-esteem problems." Anxiety alone can cause a lot of discomfort, pain, stiffness, and trouble with daily activities, according to Amanda Baker, director of the Center for Anxiety and Traumatic Stress Disorders in the Department of Psychiatry at Massachusetts General Hospital.

The roots of Somatic Therapy can be traced back to the early 20th century to Wilhelm Reich, a student of Sigmund Freud. Reich proposed that trauma manifests in the body as inflammation, pain, and muscular tension. His pioneering work laid the foundation for understanding the body's role in storing emotional experiences. Later, therapists like Peter Levine and Pat Ogden built upon Reich's concepts, developing comprehensive approaches to Somatic Therapy. Levine's Somatic Experiencing® and Ogden's Sensorimotor Psychotherapy have become cornerstone methods in the field, offering specialized techniques to address trauma and stress.

Early energy practitioners, such as Dr. Dolores Krieger RN, PhD, who developed Therapeutic Touch in the 1970s, Barbara Brennan, a NASA research scientist who studied CORE energetics with Dr. John Pierrakos before creating the Barbara Brennan School of Healing, and Janet Mentgen RN, BSN, a nurse in Colorado who created an energy certification program called the Healing Touch Program, have significantly impacted healthcare and private practices. Their work, which became popular in the 1980s, led to thousands of nurses, massage therapists, and lay healers gaining certifications and practicing their healing skills. This has not only enriched the field of healthcare but also provided alternative healing methods for the lay public. I had the privilege to work with Krieger, Brennan, and Mentgen and was an energy practitioner and instructor in the Healing Touch Program from the beginning.

Donna Eden, a pioneer in Energy Medicine, wrote her groundbreaking book based on her healing work in the 1990s. Together with her husband, Dr. David Feinstein, they opened Western Medicine to the concept of energy healing, aiding physical, emotional, and spiritual healing.

What do all these healing practitioners have in common? When you bring the energetic field into balance, the body, mind, and spirit also balance. We are spiritual beings who happen to be having a physical experience called life. The energetic field may be invisible to most people, but that does not deny its presence. In Somatic Therapy, we recognize the integration of body, mind, and spirit as one, not as three separate entities. These healers show how Somatic Therapy works Vibrationally!

Somatic Therapy stands on the shoulders of all these pioneers who have helped us see that we are whole beings - body/mind/spirit. The primary goals are straightforward yet quite profound. Practitioners aim to reduce physical symptoms related to stress and trauma by helping you become more aware of your body's signals. This heightened awareness through using Somatic Therapy leads to better emotional regulation, making it easier to manage stress and anxiety. Additionally, Somatic Therapy enhances resilience, equipping you with the tools to bounce back from life's challenges more effectively. By addressing both the physical and emotional aspects of well-being, Somatic Therapy offers a comprehensive approach to healing.

What is most exciting is the cutting-edge brain science that people like Dr. Joe Dispensa, Dr. Daniel Amen with the Amen clinics, and many others are showing exactly how thoughts and emotions can be changed or released in the brain. These writers refer to this as the neuroplasticity of the brain. Their science shows how Somatic Therapy works physiologically!

Somatic Therapy has several forms, each with unique methods and applications. Somatic Experiencing®, developed by Peter Levine, focuses on helping clients tolerate and accept physical sensations related to trauma. This method aims to modify trauma-related stress responses, promoting long-term healing. Sensorimotor Psychotherapy, founded by Pat Ogden, helps clients distinguish between trauma-based emotions and physical sensations, providing a more straightforward path to emotional regulation. Bioenergetic Analysis, another influential method, assesses and intervenes in the emotional realm through bodily movement, offering a dynamic approach to emotional and physical balance. Energy balancing taught in the Brennan school, the Healing Touch program, and energy medicine show how trapped stress in the physical and emotional body can be released and rebalanced.

It's important to remember that "Somatic Therapy" is a general term encompassing many wellness approaches. So, as you explore Somatic Therapy, you'll discover that it's not a one-size-fits-all approach. Each method offers unique benefits, allowing you to find the techniques that resonate most with your experiences and needs. Whether through breathwork, mindfulness, or therapeutic movement, Somatic Therapy provides a versatile toolkit for enhancing your well-being. Integrating these practices into your daily life allows you to achieve a harmonious balance between mind and body, paving the way for lasting emotional and physical health.

THE SCIENCE BEHIND THE MIND-BODY CONNECTION

The connection between our mind and body is more than just a poetic notion; it's a well-documented scientific reality. At the heart of this relationship lies the autonomic nervous system, which regulates involuntary bodily functions such as heartbeat, digestion, and respiratory rate. The autonomic nervous system has two main branches: the sympathetic and the parasympathetic nervous systems. The sympathetic nervous system is known as the "fight, flight or freeze" system because it prepares the body to respond to perceived threats by increasing heart rate, dilating airways, and releasing stress hormones like adrenaline. Conversely, the parasympathetic nervous system is called the "rest and digest" system. It promotes relaxation and recovery by slowing the heart rate, enhancing digestion, and conserving energy.

When we experience stress or trauma, the autonomic nervous system can become dysregulated. Prolonged activation of the sympathetic nervous system leads to chronic stress, which can manifest as physical symptoms such as headaches, muscle tension, and digestive issues. The concept of body memory comes into play with this understanding. Our bodies hold onto memories, especially traumatic ones, in ways that can affect our physical and emotional health. For example, someone who has experienced a traumatic event might develop chronic back pain or digestive problems, even if they don't consciously connect these symptoms to their past experiences. Research supports the idea that trauma-related impressions bypass our conscious mind and manifest as psychosomatic symptoms, a concept initially proposed by Pierre Janet, a pioneering figure in the field of psychology.

Bessel van der Kolk, MD, author of The Body Keeps the Score, refers to specialized brain scans that show the two halves of the brain do not speak the same language. Images of past trauma activate the right hemisphere of the brain and deactivate the left. The right and left sides of the brain also process the imprints of the past in very different ways. Your left brain remembers statistics and the vocabulary of events. The right brain stores memories of sound, touch, smell, and the emotions they evoke. So, people who are very upset sometimes say they are "losing their minds." Van der Kolk points out that they are experiencing a loss of executive functioning. So, when something triggers a past memory for traumatized people, they react as if the traumatic event were happening right now, thanks to their right brain. However, since their left brain isn't working so well, they may not realize their reaction is to the past. All they know is that they are angry, terrified, enraged, ashamed, or frozen. Later, after the outburst, they may look to blame someone or something for their emotional storm.

One of the most compelling theories that explain the mind-body connection is the polyvagal theory, developed by Stephen Porges. This theory describes the autonomic nervous system's role in regulating social behavior, emotional expression, and psychological experience. According to polyvagal theory, the autonomic nervous system has three stages: social communication, mobilization (fight or flight), and immobilization-freeze (feigning death). In mammals, a specific nerve called the myelinated vagus nerve connects the heart with the muscles of the face and head, enabling social interactions to regulate our visceral state. This means that our ability to feel safe and connected with others can directly influence our physiological responses to stress.

Attachment theory, another crucial psychological framework, also highlights the mind-body connection. Initially developed by John Bowlby, attachment theory explores how early relationships with caregivers shape our emotional and psychological development. Secure attachments in childhood can lead to better emotional regulation and resilience in adulthood, while insecure attachments can contribute to chronic stress and emotional dysregulation. In Somatic Therapy, understanding one's attachment style can provide valuable insights into how past relationships influence current physical and emotional health.

Empirical evidence supports the effectiveness of Somatic Therapy in addressing these complex mind-body interactions. For instance, a study conducted by Peter Levine, the developer of Somatic Experiencing®, demonstrated significant reductions in post-traumatic stress disorder (PTSD) symptoms through somatic practices. Participants reported improved emotional regulation and decreased physical symptoms such as chronic pain and muscle tension.

Another study reviewed by the National Institutes of Health found that Somatic Therapy techniques like mindfulness, grounding, and movement therapy can effectively alleviate mental health issues, including PTSD and anxiety. These findings are further supported by case studies showcasing successful outcomes. For example, one case study involved a woman who had suffered from chronic headaches for years. Through Somatic Therapy, she learned to recognize and release the tension held in her body, leading to significant relief and improved well-being.

The scientific principles underpinning Somatic Therapy offer a robust framework for understanding how our bodies and minds are intricately connected. By addressing both physical sensations and emotional experiences, Somatic Therapy provides a holistic approach to healing that can bring profound and lasting relief. Whether it's through understanding the role of the autonomic nervous system, exploring the concept of body memory, or delving into theories like polyvagal theory and attachment theory, the science behind Somatic Therapy underscores its potential to transform lives.

KEY PRINCIPLES OF SOMATIC THERAPY

Somatic Therapy rests on several core principles guiding its practice, ensuring it addresses the mind and body in harmony. One of the foundational concepts is the importance of body awareness and mindfulness. Imagine you are standing in the woods, perhaps sitting on a log or rock. Tune in to the sounds of the breeze blowing in the trees, the distant sounds of birds chirping, or squirrels running in the treetops. You feel the breeze across your face, the texture of the log against your legs, and you smell the decaying leaves around you. Being present in the moment and aware of your body, this type of mindfulness forms the bedrock of Somatic Therapy. By fostering this awareness, you learn to recognize the physical sensations associated with stress and trauma, thus opening the door to healing.

Another crucial principle is the role of the therapist-client relationship. This dynamic is not just about one person providing solutions and the other receiving them. Instead, it's a collaborative effort where the therapist offers a safe, empathetic space for you to explore your experiences. The trust built in this relationship allows for deeper emotional and physical healing. Picture yourself sitting across from a therapist who listens intently to your words and your body's subtle cues. This attentive presence helps you feel understood and supported, making navigating your healing process easier. It's important to point out that Somatic Therapy is not talk therapy. Practitioners are generally not psychotherapists or psychiatrists. However, they are trained to listen to the body's cues. What happens in a Somatic Therapy healing session?

The therapeutic process in Somatic Therapy involves several key steps. Initially, there is an assessment phase where you and your therapist set clear goals. This might include discussing your history, identifying areas of tension in your body, and understanding the emotions tied to these physical sensations. Various techniques are employed to help you reconnect with your body. Grounding exercises, for instance, involve simple actions like feeling your feet firmly planted on the ground or holding a textured object. Centering techniques include deep breathing or visualizing a calm place. Another method, known as titration, involves gradually exposing yourself to traumatic memories in small, manageable doses. This helps you process these memories without becoming overwhelmed.

Safety and stabilization are paramount in Somatic Therapy. Creating a secure environment ensures you feel comfortable exploring your deepest emotions and physical sensations. Techniques to ensure safety include setting clear boundaries, using calming sensory inputs like soft lighting or soothing music, and employing practices that help you return to relax if you start feeling overwhelmed. Stabilization is building a solid foundation before diving into more challenging work. This may involve practicing mindfulness and grounding exercises regularly so you have reliable tools to manage stress and anxiety.

The concept of titration in trauma therapy is particularly significant. Titration means taking things slowly and breaking down traumatic experiences into small, digestible pieces. For instance, if you have a traumatic memory that causes anxiety, your therapist might start by having you focus on a less intense aspect of that memory. You might recall a neutral part of the event, like the color of the walls in the room where it happened. Gradually, you build up to more challenging parts of the memory, always ensuring you remain within a manageable level of emotional intensity. This method helps prevent overwhelming emotions and allows for more effective processing of trauma.

An example of a titration exercise might be if you fear driving due to a past accident. Instead of jumping straight into driving, you might start by sitting in a parked car, focusing on your breath and the sensation of the seat beneath you. Over time, you might turn on the engine and drive short distances while monitoring your physical and emotional responses. The benefits of titration are immense; it helps you build resilience, manage overwhelming sensations, and gradually reclaim parts of your life that have been overshadowed by trauma.

By understanding and embracing these fundamental principles, you can navigate the complexities of Somatic Therapy with greater confidence and clarity. The healing journey becomes less daunting when you have a clear roadmap and supportive practices to guide you through.

HOW SOMATIC THERAPY COMPLEMENTS OTHER HOLISTIC PRACTICES

Integrating Somatic Therapy with mindfulness techniques can enhance both practices, creating a powerful synergy for healing. Take mindful breathing exercises, for example. When you consciously focus on your breath, you bring awareness to the present moment. This simple act can help you tune into your body's sensations, making identifying areas of tension or discomfort easier. Combining mindful breathing with somatic awareness can deepen your connection to your body and mind. Imagine sitting in a quiet room, closing your eyes, and taking slow, deep breaths. As you inhale, you notice the rise of your chest and the expansion of your abdomen. As you exhale, you become aware of the subtle release of tension in your shoulders and neck. This practice calms your mind and helps you develop a greater awareness of your body's needs.

Similarly, body scanning techniques can be enhanced by incorporating somatic principles. A body scan involves mentally scanning your body from head to toe, paying attention to any sensations you encounter. By adding somatic awareness to this practice, you can identify and address physical symptoms of stress or trauma more effectively. For instance, you might notice a tightness in your lower back while performing a body scan. Instead of simply acknowledging the sensation, you can use somatic techniques to explore the underlying emotions or memories associated with it. This deeper awareness can lead to more profound healing and emotional release.

The synergy between Somatic Therapy and yoga is another example of how these practices complement each other. Yoga emphasizes body awareness and mindful movement, making it a natural partner for somatic techniques. By incorporating somatic awareness into your yoga practice, you can enhance the benefits of each pose. For example, in a simple forward fold, you can focus on the sensations in your hamstrings and lower back, noticing any areas of tension or discomfort. You can make minor adjustments to your alignment by tuning into these sensations, deepening the stretch, and promoting more significant release. Combining yoga with somatic exercises can also help you develop a more intuitive understanding of your body's needs, allowing you to adapt your practice to suit your unique physical and emotional state.

Somatic Therapy also plays a significant role in energy healing, working with energy-based practices to promote balance and well-being. For example, healing techniques found in Healing Touch, Reiki, acupuncture, and chakra balancing will focus on aligning and balancing the body's energy. Incorporating somatic exercises into these practices can enhance energy flow throughout your body. For instance, during a Healing Touch session, you might use somatic techniques to become more aware of the sensations in your body, helping you identify areas where energy is blocked or stagnant. Focusing on these areas and using somatic exercises to release tension can promote a more balanced and harmonious energy flow.

Aromatherapy is another holistic practice that can be seamlessly integrated with Somatic Therapy. Essential oils have long been used to promote relaxation, balance emotions, and support overall well-being. By incorporating aromatherapy into your somatic practice, you can enhance the effectiveness of both modalities. For instance, you might choose essential oils like lavender, Roman chamomile, or citrus oils like orange or bergamot for their calming and grounding properties. During a Somatic Therapy session, you can diffuse these oils in the room or apply them topically to pulse points or to the soles of the feet. The soothing aroma can help you relax and become more present, making it easier to tune into your body's sensations and release tension. Another method is to create a personalized blend of oils tailored to your specific needs, using them during your somatic exercises to support your emotional and physical well-being.

By integrating Somatic Therapy with these holistic practices, you can create a comprehensive and practical approach to healing. Each practice complements the others, enhancing their benefits and providing a more profound and lasting impact. Whether focusing on mindfulness, yoga, energy healing, or aromatherapy, incorporating somatic techniques can help you achieve excellent balance, release stored trauma, and promote overall well-being.

COMMON MISCONCEPTIONS ABOUT SOMATIC THERAPY

One common misconception about Somatic Therapy is that it's purely physical, focusing only on the body without considering the mind, which is not valid. Somatic Therapy is a holistic approach that integrates mind and body to foster healing and well-being. It recognizes that our emotions and psychological states are deeply intertwined with physical experiences. For instance, during a Somatic Therapy session, you might be guided to focus on a physical sensation like tightness in your chest. As you explore this sensation, you may uncover underlying emotions such as anxiety or sadness. By addressing physical and emotional components, Somatic Therapy helps you achieve a more profound and lasting healing.

To illustrate, imagine you're feeling overwhelmed by stress at work. You notice your shoulders are tense, and your jaw is clenched. In a Somatic Therapy session, you might be guided to gently relax these areas while exploring the thoughts and feelings contributing to your stress. This dual focus on body and mind allows you to release tension and gain insight into your emotional state. It's not just about relaxing your muscles; it's about understanding and addressing the root causes of your stress. This holistic approach ensures that you're not merely treating symptoms but fostering overall well-being. Combined with some energy work, the therapist may also brush the tension (felt as congested or thick energy) out of the field over the area where you are experiencing discomfort.

Another myth is that Somatic Therapy lacks scientific backing. In reality, there is a growing body of evidence supporting its efficacy. Numerous studies have demonstrated the effectiveness of Somatic Therapy in treating various conditions, including post-traumatic stress disorder (PTSD), anxiety, and chronic pain. For example, a study published in the Journal of Traumatic Stress found that participants who underwent Somatic Therapy experienced significant reductions in PTSD symptoms. The study highlighted how somatic techniques helped participants process traumatic memories and reduce physical symptoms associated with trauma. Additionally, reputable health organizations like the American Psychological Association have recognized the benefits of Somatic Therapy, further validating its scientific credibility.

Many people also believe that Somatic Therapy is only for those who have experienced severe trauma. While it's true that Somatic Therapy is incredibly effective for trauma survivors, it can benefit anyone, regardless of the severity of their experiences. Even if you're dealing with everyday stress and anxiety, Somatic Therapy can offer valuable tools for managing these challenges. For instance, if you often feel anxious in social situations, somatic techniques like grounding and mindful breathing can help you stay calm and present. Success stories abound from individuals with various backgrounds who have found relief and healing through Somatic Therapy, whether they were dealing with minor stressors or significant trauma.

Another misconception is that Somatic Therapy is a quick fix. Healing takes time and commitment, especially deep-seated emotional and physical issues. Somatic Therapy requires ongoing practice and patience. It's not about a one-time solution but creating lasting changes through consistent effort. For example, someone with chronic pain might initially notice minor improvements after a few sessions. Over time, these improvements can become more pronounced and sustainable with regular practice of somatic techniques. The long-term benefits of Somatic Therapy include reducing physical symptoms and enhancing emotional resilience and overall well-being.

Patience and commitment are crucial in Somatic Therapy. It's a process that unfolds gradually, allowing you to build a deeper connection with your body and mind over time. Think of it as tending to a garden. You don't plant seeds and expect a full bloom the next day. Instead, you nurture the soil, water the plants, and give them time to grow. Similarly, Somatic Therapy involves:

- Nurturing your body and mind.
- Practicing techniques regularly.
- Allowing time for healing to take root.

The rewards are worth the effort—greater emotional balance, reduced stress, and a more harmonious relationship with your body.

In summary, Somatic Therapy is a holistic and scientifically supported approach that benefits a wide range of individuals, not just those with severe trauma. It requires ongoing practice and patience, promising profound and lasting benefits. This therapy offers a unique and effective way to address physical and emotional well-being, making it a valuable addition to your self-care toolkit. As you explore the practices and principles outlined in this book, remember that healing is a journey unfolding with each mindful breath and gentle movement. By embracing Somatic Therapy, you're taking an essential step toward a more balanced, peaceful, and fulfilling life.

CHAPTER TWO

GETTING STARTED WITH SOMATIC THERAPY

It was a sunny afternoon when I first met Al at a community wellness event. He had just turned 60 and was feeling overwhelmed by the physical and emotional changes that come with aging. He shared how difficult it was to find balance amidst the daily stresses and emotional upheavals. As we talked, I realized how many men over 50, like Al, could benefit from a structured approach to preparing their minds and bodies for Somatic Therapy. This chapter is dedicated to helping you build that foundation, ensuring you're mentally and physically ready for the healing ahead.

PREPARING YOUR MIND AND BODY FOR HEALING

Your mindset is pivotal in how effectively you can embrace somatic therapy. A positive attitude, rooted in self-compassion and patience, sets the stage for meaningful progress. Cultivating a positive mindset involves several techniques. Begin by practicing gratitude daily; take a moment each morning to reflect on three things you're thankful for. I recommend writing down your three "gratitudes" in a gratitude journal at your bedside, where you will see them. This simple act can shift your focus from what's lacking to what's abundant in your life. Another technique is to engage in affirmations. These are positive statements about yourself that you repeat daily. They might initially feel awkward, but over time, they can reshape your internal dialogue and reinforce self-worth. I'm a big promoter of positive affirmations and sticky notes! The bathroom mirror, the kitchen refrigerator, the computer, the dashboard of your car, or anywhere else you frequent daily in your home or car.

The role of self-compassion can't be overstated. Being kind to yourself, especially when things don't go as planned, is crucial. Studies have shown that self-compassion reduces stress and improves emotional well-being. Remember, healing is a gradual process, and taking small steps is okay. Patience is your ally in this journey; celebrate the small victories and understand that setbacks are part of the growth. Within every adversity is the seed of growth! Setbacks or perceived failures are only feedback saying, "Not this way, there's a better way!"

Physical preparation is equally important. Your body needs to be in a receptive state for somatic practices to be effective. Begin with gentle stretches to release tension. Focus on areas like your neck, shoulders, and lower back—common spots where stress accumulates. A simple routine might involve neck rolls, shoulder shrugs, and gentle twists. These movements help increase blood flow and flexibility, preparing your body for more profound work. Hydration and nutrition also play crucial roles. Drinking plenty of water keeps your tissues hydrated, making it easier for your body to release tension. Eating a balanced diet rich in fruits, vegetables, and lean proteins provides the necessary nutrients for optimal body function. Avoid excessive caffeine and sugar, which increase stress and hinder your progress. As an avid black tea consumer, I have learned to love plain, unadulterated herbal teas and decaffeinated black tea!

Relaxation techniques are integral to priming your body for Somatic Therapy. Deep breathing exercises, such as diaphragmatic breathing, can calm your nervous system and make you more receptive to healing. To practice this:

1. Sit comfortably and place one hand on your chest and the other on your abdomen.
2. Inhale deeply through your nose, allowing your abdomen to rise more than your chest.
3. Exhale slowly through your mouth pursing your lips as if blowing through a straw, feeling your abdomen fall. This simple exercise can reduce anxiety and improve focus.

I love this particular breathing exercise best. I literally can feel the stress leave my body.

Progressive muscle relaxation is another effective technique. Tense each muscle group from your toes for five seconds, then release. Work your way up to your head, paying attention to the sensations of tension and relaxation. Meditation is another powerful tool. Even a few minutes of mindfulness meditation daily can significantly reduce stress and enhance emotional resilience. Find a quiet spot, close your eyes, and focus on your breath. Let go of any distractions and bring your attention to your breath whenever your mind wanders. More on meditation later.

Consistency is vital in Somatic Therapy. Regular practice not only enhances the effectiveness of the techniques but also ingrains them into your daily routine. Set a schedule for your practice. It doesn't have to be long; even 10-15 minutes daily can make a significant difference. Please choose a time that works best for you, whether first thing in the morning or before bed. Tracking your progress can help you stay motivated. Keep a journal to note your daily practices, any sensations or emotions you experience, and how you feel afterward. This lets you see your progress and identify patterns and areas needing more focus. Over time, this practice becomes a cherished part of your day, a moment of peace and self-care amidst the busyness of life.

Reflection Section

Take a few minutes to reflect on your current mindset and physical state. How do you feel about your readiness for Somatic Therapy? What areas of your life could benefit from more self-compassion and patience? Write down one or two practical steps this week to prepare your mind and body for healing.

By taking these steps to prepare your mind and body, you're setting a solid foundation for the healing practices that follow. The journey to well-being is not a sprint but a marathon that requires patience, consistency, and a compassionate approach to yourself.

SETTING INTENTIONS FOR YOUR SOMATIC JOURNEY

Setting intentions is a powerful tool in Somatic Therapy. It helps guide your actions and thoughts toward a meaningful goal. Unlike goals, which are specific and measurable, intentions are broader and more about the journey than the destination. Think of intentions as the guiding star that aligns you with your values and desires. For example, while a goal might be to practice mindfulness for 10 minutes each day, an intention could be to cultivate a sense of peace and presence in your daily life. This subtle shift in focus from achieving to being can significantly affect your somatic healing process.

To set personal intentions, start with some reflective exercises. Find a quiet space where you can sit comfortably and undisturbed. Close your eyes and take a few deep breaths to center yourself. Begin by asking yourself what you truly need at this moment in your life. Is it more peace, better emotional balance, or a deeper connection with your body? Write down whatever comes to mind without judgment. Look for common themes once you have a list of needs and desires. These themes will help you craft your intentions. For instance, if your reflections reveal a need for emotional balance, your intention might be, "I aim to nurture emotional stability and resilience."

Writing and verbalizing your intentions can reinforce them. Once you have identified your intentions, write them down in a journal or on a piece of paper you can keep in a visible place. This act of writing helps solidify your commitment. Say your intentions out loud each day, preferably in the morning. Verbalizing them can make them feel more natural and actionable. For example, saying, "I intend to approach each day with a calm and focused mind," sets a positive tone for your day and aligns your actions with your intentions.

Visualization is another effective technique for reinforcing your intentions. Visualization involves creating a mental image of your desired outcome. To practice this, find a comfortable position, close your eyes, and take a few deep breaths. Imagine yourself living out your intention. To cultivate peace, visualize a peaceful scene, such as a serene beach or a quiet forest. Picture yourself in this place, feeling calm and relaxed. Engage all your senses in this visualization—imagine the sound of the waves, the smell of the ocean, and the feel of the sand beneath your feet. Or imagine the sound of birds in the forest, the smell of the earth, and the feel of leaves and rocks beneath your shoes. The benefits of visualizing successful outcomes are substantial. It reinforces your intentions and trains your mind to recognize and create these desired states in your daily life.

Intentions, dreams, and visions for your life are not set in stone. They can and should be revisited and refined as needed. Your needs and desires may evolve as you progress in your Somatic Therapy practice. Regular reflection can help you stay aligned with your current state. Journaling is an excellent tool for this ongoing reflection. Set aside weekly time to review your intentions and write about your experiences. Note any changes in your emotional or physical well-being and how your intentions have influenced these changes. If you find that an intention no longer resonates with you, don't hesitate to adjust it. For instance, if your original intention was to cultivate peace, but you now feel a stronger need for emotional resilience, modify your intention to reflect this shift. Techniques for adjusting intentions include adding new elements, removing outdated aspects, or rephrasing them to better align with your current state.

I have a comfortable chair in my office by a window. There is a small table next to my chair with my vision for my life three years into the future written out that I would love. Why three years into the future? Well, if I said one year from now, my mind would say, "Wait a minute, I don't believe you can do that!" But three years into the future, my brain isn't sure and is willing to go along with it. So, each morning before I start my busy day, I sit and read my vision, visualizing myself living my dream three years into the future. Then I feel the emotions of actually being that person in the future. Next, I reflect on what small baby steps I could take that day to achieve my vision. Does my vision change over time? Yes, life changes, and so do dreams.

Setting, visualizing, and revisiting your intentions creates a dynamic and flexible framework for your Somatic Therapy practice. This approach provides direction and fosters a deeper connection with yourself and your healing process.

CREATING A SAFE AND SACRED SPACE FOR PRACTICE

Imagine having a cozy corner in your home where you can retreat away from the hustle and bustle of everyday life. A dedicated practice space can significantly enhance your Somatic Therapy experience. It's not just about having a physical location; it's about creating an environment that fosters healing and introspection. Consistency in using this space can provide psychological benefits, stability, and routine. When you have a designated area for your practice, it becomes easier to slip into a state of relaxation and focus. The space should be physically comfortable—think soft cushions, a supportive chair, or a yoga mat. Privacy is crucial, too; you need a place where you won't be interrupted, so consider choosing a room with a door you can close or a secluded outdoor spot.

Setting up a healing environment doesn't have to be complicated. Start by decluttering the area. A clutter-free space can help clear your mind and make it easier to focus on your practice. Organize the space so that everything you need is within arm's reach. Lighting, plants, and soothing colors can transform a simple space into a sanctuary. Candles provide a warm, calming glow, while plants can bring a touch of nature indoors, enhancing your connection to the earth. Colors like soft blues, greens, and earthy tones can promote relaxation and peace. You don't need to redecorate your entire home; small changes can make a big difference.

Sensory elements play a significant role in enhancing your practice. Aromatherapy, for instance, can be incredibly soothing. Essential oils like lavender, chamomile, and eucalyptus are known for their calming effects. You can use a diffuser to spread these scents throughout your space, apply a few drops to your wrists, and inhale deeply. Calming sounds or music can also help set the tone for your practice. Consider playing soft instrumental music and nature sounds like flowing water or birdsong, or even use guided meditations. The goal is to create an environment that engages your senses and helps you relax.

Ensuring the space feels safe and supportive is paramount. Emotional and physical safety are the cornerstones of effective Somatic Therapy. Start by creating boundaries to prevent interruptions. Let your family or housemates know this is your time and space for healing, and kindly ask them to respect it. Personalizing the space with meaningful objects can also make it more supportive. This might include photos of loved ones, inspirational quotes, or sentimental items. These objects can serve as reminders of your intentions and the support you have in your life.

Your sacred space should reflect you and what brings you peace and comfort. It's not about following a strict set of rules but about creating an environment that feels right for you. Spend some time in your space and notice how it makes you feel. Adjust it as needed until it feels just right. Whether adding a cozy blanket, a favorite book, or a piece of art that inspires you, these small touches can make your space uniquely yours.

Reflection Section

Take a moment to consider what elements make you feel calm and supported. Write down a list of items you already have at home that could be incorporated into your sacred space. Think about where you could create this space—maybe it's a quiet corner of your bedroom, a spot in your garden, or even a small area in your living room. Spend a few minutes visualizing this space and how it will feel once it's set up.

Creating a safe and sacred space for practice is an act of self-care. It's a way to honor your commitment to healing and create a sanctuary to reconnect with yourself. By taking the time to set up this space, you're not only enhancing your Somatic Therapy practice but also creating a haven of peace and tranquility in your home.

TOOLS AND RESOURCES TO SUPPORT YOUR PRACTICE

When beginning your Somatic Therapy practice, having the right tools can make a world of difference. Let's start with the basics. A yoga mat provides a comfortable and supportive surface for various exercises and stretches. If you have issues with your back or knees, consider adding cushions or bolsters. These can help you maintain proper alignment and support during your practice. Journals are another invaluable tool. They allow you to document your experiences, track your progress, and reflect on your emotional and physical state. Write freely about your sensations, emotions, and any insights you gain during your sessions.

Books, websites, and apps can offer additional support and guidance. For reading, consider titles like "Waking the Tiger" by Peter Levine and "The Body Keeps the Score" by Bessel van der Kolk. These books provide deep insights into the principles of somatic therapy. Websites like Somatic Experiencing® (https//.trauma-healing.org) offer articles, resources, and practitioner directories. Apps like BrainTap and Calm can assist with mindfulness and relaxation techniques, providing guided meditations and breathing exercises at your fingertips. These resources can reinforce your practice and offer new techniques to explore. I recently subscribed to an app with meditations, relaxing music for restfulness or sleep, and inspirational messages created by John Assaraf. He and many other modern, inspiring thought leaders speak on the app called Innercise®.

Digital tools can significantly enhance your somatic therapy experience. Online guided meditations and tutorials can provide structure and guidance, especially if you're new to the practice. Websites like YouTube host numerous free videos that guide you through various somatic exercises and mindfulness practices. Downloadable practice worksheets can help you stay organized and focused. These worksheets might include daily checklists, emotional tracking logs, and intention-setting templates. Keeping digital copies of these documents allows you to access them anytime, at home or on the go.

Exploring additional modalities can also enrich your Somatic Therapy practice. Acupuncture and massage are excellent complementary therapies that can help release physical tension and promote relaxation. Acupuncture involves the insertion of thin needles into specific points on the body to balance energy flow, while massage uses hands-on techniques to manipulate muscles and tissues. Both methods can enhance your body awareness and support the release of stored tension. Workshops and retreats focused on somatic healing provide immersive experiences where you can deepen your practice, learn new techniques, and connect with others on a similar path. Look for local events or travel to destinations known for their holistic wellness programs. These experiences can offer fresh perspectives and renewed motivation for your ongoing practice.

Remember, the tools and resources you choose should resonate with you. There's no one-size-fits-all approach, so feel free to experiment and find what works best for you. Whether it's a cozy corner with your favorite cushions, a quiet space with soothing music, or a comprehensive library of books and apps, these tools can meaningfully support and enhance your somatic therapy practice.

ESTABLISHING A SUPPORT NETWORK

When I first started exploring Somatic Therapy, I quickly realized the incredible value of having a support network. Sharing our experiences within a supportive community can provide immense emotional benefits. Connecting with others who understand what you're going through can lighten the emotional load. Knowing that you're not alone can be incredibly comforting. Moreover, a support network can motivate you to keep going, especially when you feel like giving up. Hearing others' stories of progress and resilience can inspire you to stay committed to your healing process.

Finding or creating a support group can be a game-changer. Local community groups and classes are great places to start. Check out wellness centers, libraries, or community bulletin boards for list-ings. Yoga studios and holistic health centers often host support groups centered around mindfulness and healing practices. If face-to-face interactions are challenging due to location or time constraints, online forums and social media groups can provide a similar sense of community. Facebook offers numerous groups where you can join discussions, share resources, and connect with like-minded individuals. Virtual spaces can be just as supportive and engaging as in-person groups.

Professional support is another crucial element of your Somatic Therapy practice. Seeking help from therapists and practitioners specializing in Somatic Therapy can provide expert guidance tailored to your unique needs. Finding a qualified somatic therapist might seem daunting, but there are resources to help you. Websites like the Somatic Experiencing® Trauma Institute (traumahealing.org) offer directories of certified therapists. Professional guidance can help you navigate complex emotions and physical sensations more quickly and confidently. Therapists can provide personalized techniques and adjustments, ensuring your practice is effective and safe. They can also provide a structured environment for your healing, making it easier to stay on track. Another source is https://healingtouchprogram.com, which can help you find Healing Touch practitioners in your area.

Maintaining supportive relationships within your network is essential for long-term success. Regular check-ins with support group members can help you stay connected and engaged. Whether a weekly coffee meet-up or a monthly Zoom call, these check-ins provide opportunities to share your progress, challenges, and insights. Open communication is key. Don't hesitate to share your experiences, both positive and negative. Vulnerability fosters deeper connections and allows others to offer meaningful support. This reciprocal sharing can create a strong sense of community and mutual encouragement.

In addition to group interactions, nurturing one-on-one relationships within your support network can be incredibly beneficial. Having a "healing buddy" or "success partner" can make a significant difference. This could be a friend, neighbor, family member, or church member interested in somatic therapy. You can practice techniques together, share resources, and provide each other with accountability. These one-on-one connections can offer more personalized support and understanding, making your healing process feel less isolating.

As you build and maintain your support network, remember it's a dynamic and evolving process. People's availability and interests may change, and that's okay. Be open to welcoming new members into your network and exploring different ways to connect. Flexibility and adaptability will help you sustain a robust and supportive community.

Support networks provide emotional and practical support and contribute to a sense of belonging and community. They remind us that healing doesn't have to be a solitary endeavor. We can find strength, inspiration, and resilience by connecting with others and sharing our journeys. Whether through local groups, online forums, or professional guidance, building a support network is a decisive step toward holistic well-being.

This chapter explored how to prepare your mind and body, set intentions, create a sacred space, gather tools, and establish a support network. With these foundations in place, you can dive deeper into the specific techniques and practices that will guide your healing. In the next chapter, let's move forward to uncover the transformative power of body awareness techniques.

CHAPTER THREE

BODY AWARENESS TECHNIQUES

I remember conversing with my friend Carol, a vibrant woman in her early forties. She had always been active, enjoying long walks and gardening. But over the past few years, she started feeling disconnected from her body. Stress from work and family obligations had taken a toll, leaving her with chronic aches and a sense of unease. One day, she mentioned feeling like she was going through the motions, not truly living in her body. Many of us experience this sense of disconnection, especially as we age. But body awareness can change that.

THE IMPORTANCE OF BODY AWARENESS

Body awareness, or kinesthesia, is the ability to be conscious and connected to your physical sensations and movements. It involves tuning into your body's signals, understanding their meaning, and responding appropriately. This awareness is a cornerstone of somatic therapy, as it helps bridge the gap between physical sensations and emotional health. When you become more aware of your body's messages, you can better understand how stress, trauma, or even daily life affects you. This understanding is crucial for healing, allowing you to address issues at their root rather than just treating the symptoms.

Increased body awareness has numerous benefits for overall well-being. One of the most significant advantages is the reduction in stress and anxiety. When you are in tune with your body, you can identify early signs of stress, such as muscle tension or shallow breathing, and take steps to alleviate them before they escalate. This proactive approach can prevent stress from accumulating and causing more severe issues. Additionally, body awareness improves emotional regulation and resilience. You can develop healthier coping mechanisms by recognizing how your body reacts to different emotions. For example, if you notice that your shoulders tense up when you're anxious, you can practice relaxation techniques to release that tension, helping you manage your anxiety more effectively.

The relationship between body awareness and mindfulness is also worth exploring. Mindfulness involves being present and fully engaged at the moment, and body awareness practices complement this perfectly. When you focus on your physical sensations, you naturally become more mindful. Mindful movement, such as yoga or Tai Chi, is a great way to enhance body awareness. These practices encourage you to pay attention to how your body feels as you move, helping you stay grounded in the present moment. This focus on the body can enhance your overall mindfulness practice, making it easier to maintain present-moment awareness throughout your day.

Real-life examples can illustrate the transformative power of body awareness. Take the case of Angela, a woman in her late fifties who suffered from chronic back pain for years. Traditional treatments provided little relief, so she decided to explore Somatic Therapy. By practicing body awareness techniques, Angela learned to identify the emotional triggers that exacerbated her pain. She discovered that her back pain often flared up during stressful situations at work. By addressing these emotional triggers and incorporating relaxation techniques, Angela significantly reduced her pain and improved her quality of life.

Another testimonial comes from Maria, a reader who struggled with emotional health issues. She often felt overwhelmed by anxiety and found it challenging to manage her emotions. Through consistent practice of body awareness techniques, Maria learned to recognize the physical signs of her anxiety, such as a racing heart and tight chest. By addressing these physical sensations with breathwork and mindful movement, she gained better control over her anxiety and felt more emotionally balanced. Maria's story highlights how body awareness can improve mental and emotional well-being, providing a solid foundation for overall health.

Body awareness is a powerful tool that can enhance your well-being in numerous ways. Becoming more attuned to your physical sensations and movements can reduce stress, improve emotional regulation, and strengthen your mindfulness practice. The benefits of increased body awareness extend beyond the physical, fostering a deeper connection between your mind and body. Whether you're dealing with chronic pain or emotional health issues or want to feel more present in your daily life, body awareness techniques can offer valuable support on your path to healing.

SIMPLE EXERCISES TO ENHANCE BODY AWARENESS

Gentle stretching routines can be an excellent way to cultivate body awareness. These exercises help you become more attuned to your physical sensations and can be done almost anywhere. Begin with a simple neck stretch:

1. Sit comfortably and slowly tilt your head towards one shoulder, holding the stretch for a few breaths before switching sides.
2. Follow this with shoulder rolls, gently rotating your shoulders forward and backward.
3. Move on to a seated spinal twist; sit flat on the floor, place your right hand on your left knee, and gently twist your torso to the left, holding for a few breaths before repeating on the other side.

These stretches increase flexibility and help you tune into the nuances of your body's movements and sensations.

Walking meditation is another effective exercise for enhancing body awareness. This practice combines the benefits of physical movement with mindfulness. To start, find a quiet place where you can walk undisturbed. Begin strolling, paying attention to each step. Notice how your feet contact the ground, how your weight shifts, and how your muscles engage with each movement. As you walk, focus on the rhythm of your steps and your breath. This mindful walking helps you stay present and connected to your body, making it easier to identify areas of tension or discomfort. It's a simple yet powerful way to integrate body awareness into your daily routine.

You would be surprised to know that many people meditate in very public places like walking and biking trails. I have been lucky to have lived both in Colorado and South Carolina, where walking trails abound. Check out your area and see if there is a paved walking trail near you.

The body scan exercise is a cornerstone of body awareness practices, offering a systematic way to connect with your physical sensations. To perform a body scan:

1. Find a quiet, comfortable place to sit or lie down.
2. Close your eyes and take a few deep breaths to center yourself.
3. Focus on the top of your head, noticing any sensations or tension.
4. Slowly move your attention down to your forehead, eyes, cheeks, and jaw, pausing at each point to observe how it feels.
5. Continue this process, moving down through your neck, shoulders, arms, chest, abdomen, hips, legs, and feet.
6. Don't rush; spend at least 20-30 seconds on each area. If you notice any tension or discomfort, acknowledge it without trying to change it.

This exercise helps you become more aware of your body and promotes relaxation and stress relief.

Mindful movement exercises, such as certain yoga poses and Tai Chi movements, can further enhance body awareness. Yoga poses like the Mountain Pose, where you stand tall with your feet grounded and your body aligned, or the Warrior Pose, which involves a strong, balanced stance, are excellent for tuning into your body. These poses encourage you to focus on your alignment, balance, and breath, helping you become more aware of your physical state. Tai Chi, with its slow, deliberate movements, offers similar benefits. Practicing Tai Chi movements, like the "Wave Hands Like Clouds" move, can help you connect with your body's natural rhythms and flow. These mindful movements improve physical coordination and enhance your overall sense of well-being. Check out the many YouTube videos demonstrating the basic seven steps of Tai Chi.

It's important to offer variations for different physical abilities to ensure everyone can benefit from these exercises. For those with limited mobility or who find standing difficult for long periods, seated body awareness exercises can be just as practical. For example, seated neck rolls, shoulder shrugs, and gentle spinal twists can all be done while sitting, offering the same benefits as their standing counterparts. Additionally, incorporating body awareness into daily activities can make these practices more accessible. Simple actions like paying attention to your posture while sitting at a desk, noticing how your body feels while doing household chores, or taking a few deep breaths while waiting in line can all enhance your body awareness. These small, mindful moments can add up, helping you stay connected to your body throughout the day.

Reflection Section

Take a moment to reflect on your current level of body awareness. How often do you tune into your physical sensations? Are there specific areas of your body that frequently feel tense or uncomfortable? Write down your observations and consider incorporating one or two exercises into your daily routine. Notice how these practices impact your overall well-being and sense of connection to your body.

USING BREATHWORK TO CONNECT WITH YOUR BODY

Breath is the bridge between your mind and body, a simple yet powerful tool that can enhance your connection with yourself. You engage your lungs and autonomic nervous system when you take a deep breath. This system controls your body's automatic functions, like heartbeat and digestion, and is divided into two main branches: the sympathetic and parasympathetic nervous systems. Deep breathing activates the parasympathetic nervous system, which promotes relaxation and reduces stress. It's like flipping a switch, moving your body from a fight-flight-or-freeze state to one of rest and digest. This physiological shift calms your nervous system, lowers your heart rate, and reduces blood pressure, creating a sense of calm and well-being.

Let's explore some basic breathwork techniques that can easily be incorporated into your daily routine. Diaphragmatic breathing, also known as belly breathing, is a foundational practice. Begin by sitting or lying down in a comfortable position. Place one hand on your chest and the other on your abdomen. Inhale deeply through your nose, raising your abdomen while keeping your chest relatively still. Exhale slowly through your mouth, feeling your abdomen fall. Repeat this process for several minutes, focusing on the rise and fall of your abdomen. This technique calms your mind and helps you become more aware of how your breath moves through your body. To take this breathing to the next level, purse your lips as you breathe out.

Another effective technique is the 4-7-8 breathing method. This practice is beneficial for stress relief and promoting sleep. Start by sitting comfortably and closing your eyes. Inhale quietly through your nose for a count of four. Hold your breath for a count of seven. Exhale entirely through your mouth, making a whooshing sound for a count of eight. Repeat this cycle three to four times. The 4-7-8 method slows your heart rate and promotes relaxation, making it easier to fall asleep or calm your mind during stressful moments.

Incorporating breathwork into your daily life can be surprisingly simple and effective. For instance, you can use breathing exercises for stress relief at work. If you feel overwhelmed, practice diaphragmatic or 4-7-8 breathing at your desk for a few minutes. Close your eyes, take a deep breath, and focus on the sensation of your breath filling your lungs and leaving your body. This small break can help reset your mind, making it easier to tackle your tasks with a more precise, calmer mindset.

Breathwork can also significantly improve your sleep quality. Establish a nightly routine that includes a few minutes of deep breathing before bed. This breathwork can signal to your body that it's time to wind down and prepare for rest. Try the 4-7-8 technique or a simple diaphragmatic breathing session as you lie in bed. Focus on your breath and let go of the day's stresses, allowing yourself to drift into a peaceful sleep.

Guided breathwork exercises can provide structured support for your practice. A guided relaxation breathwork session can be an excellent way to unwind. Find a quiet, comfortable place to sit or lie down. Close your eyes and take a few deep breaths to center yourself. Inhale deeply through your nose, hold for a moment, and then exhale slowly through your mouth. As you breathe, imagine a wave of relaxation flowing through your body, starting at your head and moving down to your toes. Feel the tension melt away with each exhale, leaving you feeling calm and refreshed.

Breath-focused meditation for body awareness is another beneficial practice. Sit comfortably with your eyes closed. Begin by taking a few deep breaths to settle in. Shift your focus to your breath, noticing the sensation of the air entering and leaving your nostrils. Pay attention to how your chest and abdomen rise and fall with each breath. If your mind wanders, gently bring your focus back to your breath. This meditation enhances your body awareness and promotes a more profound sense of connection between your mind and body.

GUIDED BODY SCANNING TECHNIQUES

Guided body scans are a powerful tool for enhancing body awareness, allowing you to connect deeply with your physical sensations and uncover areas of tension and release. This practice is particularly effective because it encourages you to slow down and bring focused attention to different parts of your body. Doing so lets you identify where you might be holding stress or discomfort and take steps to alleviate it. The purpose of a guided body scan is to cultivate a mindful awareness of your body, helping you tune into subtle sensations that often go unnoticed in the hustle and bustle of daily life. This heightened awareness can lead to significant improvements in both physical and emotional well-being.

To conduct a guided body scan, find a quiet, comfortable place where you won't be disturbed. You can sit or lie down, whichever feels more relaxing for you. Close your eyes and take a few deep breaths to center yourself. Start at the top of your head, bringing your attention to your scalp. Notice any sensations—tingling, warmth, tightness. Slowly move your focus down to your forehead, eyes, cheeks, jaw, and neck, pausing at each point to observe how it feels. Continue this process, moving through your shoulders, arms, chest, abdomen, hips, legs, and feet. Don't rush; spend about 20-30 seconds on each area. If your mind wanders, gently bring your focus back to the body part you're scanning. This practice helps you become more aware of your body and promotes relaxation and stress relief.

There are several variations of body scan techniques that can keep your practice engaging and tailored to your needs. A short, focused body scan is excellent for quick relaxation. This version might take 5-10 minutes, focusing on critical areas where you tend to hold tension, such as your shoulders, neck, and lower back. A quick scan like this can be perfect during a lunch break or before a stressful meeting. On the other hand, a detailed, extended body scan offers a deeper level of awareness and can last 20-30 minutes or more. This version allows you to explore each part of your body more thoroughly, making it ideal for a more in-depth practice session, perhaps in the evening when you have more time to unwind.

For those who prefer guided assistance, numerous audio and written resources are available to support your body scan practice. Apps like Headspace and Calm offer guided body scan meditations you can follow. These apps provide various options, from short scans to extended sessions, catering to different needs and schedules. Online platforms like YouTube also host numerous guided body scan audio files, offering free access to high-quality guided meditations. These resources can be beneficial, especially if you're new to body scans or find it challenging to focus on your own.

Reflection Section

Take a moment to think about when and where you can incorporate a guided body scan into your daily routine. Write down any observations about areas of your body that often feel tense or uncomfortable. Consider trying a short, focused body scan during a break at work or an extended session in the evening. Reflect on how these practices might help you connect more deeply with your body and enhance your overall well-being.

Guided body scans are a versatile and effective way to enhance body awareness. Whether you choose a short, focused scan for quick relaxation or a detailed, extended scan for deeper understanding, these practices can provide valuable insights into your physical and emotional state. Regularly incorporating guided body scans into your routine can develop a greater sense of connection with your body, helping you manage stress and improve your overall well-being.

DEVELOPING A DAILY BODY AWARENESS ROUTINE

Consistency is vital when it comes to body awareness exercises. Regular practice is necessary to see and feel the benefits of any other skill. Setting a daily schedule for your body awareness practice can be incredibly helpful. Think of it as a commitment to yourself and your well-being. Start by identifying a time of day that works best for you. Some people find that morning is ideal, as it sets a positive tone for the rest of the day. Others may prefer the evening, using body awareness exercises to wind down and prepare for restful sleep. Whatever you choose, try to stick to it. Consistency helps build a habit, making incorporating these practices into your daily life easier.

Building body awareness into your daily routines doesn't have to be complicated. Start your day with a simple morning body scan. This scan can be done while you're still in bed or after you wake up. You can mentally scan your body from head to toe, noticing any areas of tension or discomfort. This practice helps you become more aware of your body and sets a mindful tone for the day ahead. In the evening, incorporate some breathwork for relaxation. Spend five to ten minutes practicing deep breathing exercises to calm your mind and body. This can help release any tension accumulated throughout the day and prepare you for a good night's sleep.

Maintaining motivation can be challenging, especially when life gets busy. One effective strategy is to keep a body awareness journal. Document your daily practices, noting any sensations, emotions, or changes you observe. This helps you track your progress and provides a sense of accomplishment. Celebrate your milestones, no matter how small. Acknowledging these achievements can keep you motivated, whether it's a week of consistent practice or a noticeable improvement in your well-being. Another tip is to set realistic goals. Instead of aiming for an hour of practice daily, start with ten minutes. Gradually increase the time as you become more comfortable with the routines. Remember, it's better to consistently practice for a short time than to have long, sporadic sessions.

Flexibility and adaptation are crucial for maintaining a sustainable routine. Life is unpredictable, and there will be days when sticking to your schedule feels impossible. On such days, adapt your exercises to fit your circumstances. If you're short on time, opt for a quick body scan or a few minutes of breathwork. If you're stressed, prioritize relaxation techniques over more intensive practices. The goal is to maintain a connection with your body, even if it's just for a few minutes. Modify your routines based on the seasons as well.

For instance, you might prefer indoor activities like yoga or guided body scans during the colder months. In the warmer months, take advantage of outdoor spaces for walking meditations or mindful stretching in nature.

Incorporating these practices into daily life creates a solid foundation for ongoing well-being. The benefits of regular body awareness exercises extend beyond physical health, enhancing your emotional and mental resilience. Whether you're starting your day with a body scan, practicing breathwork in the evening, or adapting exercises to fit your busy schedule, these routines can provide stability and self-care.

In this chapter, we've explored the importance of consistency in body awareness practices, provided a daily routine, and offered tips for maintaining motivation. Integrating these exercises into your daily life can enhance your overall well-being and create a solid foundation for healing. Next, we'll delve into exploring the profound benefits of releasing stored trauma, providing you with practical techniques to help you move forward.

CHAPTER FOUR

RELEASING STORED TRAUMA

A couple of years ago, I met Jane at a wellness retreat. She was in her late fifties, vibrant and full of life, yet she carried an invisible weight that seemed to burden her every step. As we talked, she shared how she had been dealing with chronic back pain for years. Despite countless doctor visits and various treatments, nothing seemed to bring lasting relief. It wasn't until she explored Somatic Therapy that she began to understand the deeper layers of her pain. Jane's story is not unique. Many people may experience similar struggles, where physical discomfort is deeply intertwined with emotional trauma.

UNDERSTANDING TRAUMA AND ITS PHYSICAL MANIFESTATIONS

Trauma leaves a lasting imprint not just on our minds but also on our bodies. When you experience a traumatic event, your body reacts by activating its fight-flight-or-freeze response, a survival mechanism designed to protect you from harm. The rational brain, your left brain, is not in sync with your emotional brain, your right brain. As a result, you are pushed outside your window of tolerance - the range of optimal functioning. You may be reactive and disorganized, and your filters seem to stop working. If you've shut down, you feel numb in body and mind, and your thinking becomes sluggish.

The nervous system, particularly the autonomic system, is crucial in this process. It consists of the sympathetic nervous system, which prepares your body to respond to danger, and the parasympathetic nervous system, which helps you calm down and recover once the threat has passed. However, when trauma is severe or prolonged, this system can become dysregulated. Your body remains in a state of heightened alert or arousal, unable to fully relax or recover. This chronic state of stress manifests physically, leading to various symptoms.

Common physical symptoms of stored trauma include chronic pain, muscle tension, headaches, and digestive issues. For example, you might find that your shoulders are always tight or suffer from frequent stomachaches without apparent medical cause. These symptoms are your body's way of signaling that something deeper needs attention. The nervous system stores these traumatic experiences, which become embedded in your muscles, tissues, and organs over time. This is why you might experience physical pain unrelated to any specific injury or condition.

Unresolved trauma can have long-term effects on your physical health. Chronic pain and tension are expected outcomes, as your muscles remain in constant contraction, and you cannot fully relax. It can lead to conditions like fibromyalgia or tension headaches. Sleep disturbances are another significant impact of unresolved trauma. You might find falling or staying asleep difficult, leading to constant fatigue. This lack of restful sleep further exacerbates physical and emotional stress, creating a vicious cycle that's hard to break. Over time, the continuous strain on your body can lead to more severe health issues, such as cardiovascular problems, weakened immune function, and even metabolic disorders.

Somatic markers are physical responses your body creates in reaction to emotional experiences. These markers are deeply connected to your emotions and can manifest in various ways. For example, muscle tightness is a standard somatic marker of anxiety or fear. You might notice your jaw clenches or your shoulders hunching when stressed. Digestive issues, such as a sudden upset stomach or loss of appetite, can also be somatic markers of emotional distress. These physical symptoms are your body's way of processing and expressing emotions you might not even be consciously aware of. The connection between somatic markers and specific emotions is profound. Understanding this connection can help you identify and address the underlying emotional triggers.

Let's look at a real-life example to illustrate how trauma manifests physically. Consider the case of Maggie, a woman who experienced chronic back pain for years without any apparent physical cause. Through Somatic Therapy, she discovered that her pain was linked to unresolved trauma from a car accident she had experienced decades ago. By addressing the emotional impact of the accident and using somatic techniques to release the stored tension, Maggie was able to reduce her back pain significantly.

Another testimonial comes from Sarah, a reader who struggled with digestive issues for most of her adult life. She had tried various diets and medical treatments with little success. It wasn't until she explored the emotional roots of her symptoms that she found relief. Through Somatic Therapy, Sarah identified that her digestive issues were linked to childhood trauma. By working through these emotional experiences and using somatic techniques to release the stored stress, she experienced significant improvements in her digestive health.

These examples highlight how deeply intertwined our physical and emotional health can be. By understanding the physiological processes involved in trauma and recognizing the signs of stored trauma in your body, you can take meaningful steps toward healing. Somatic Therapy offers practical tools and techniques to help you release stored trauma and improve both your physical and emotional well-being.

SELF-AWARENESS AND MINDFULNESS

You might ask, "How do you regain balance between your rational and emotional brains?" According to Dr. Bessel Van Der Kolk, self-awareness is the only way to achieve this and is at the very core of recovery from trauma. The technical term for this is "interoception," from the Latin meaning "look inside." Your conscious brain is primarily focused on the outside world—like getting along with others and making plans for the future. However, that does not help you manage yourself. Neuroscience research shows that the only way you can change how you feel is by becoming aware of your inner experience and learning to befriend what is happening inside yourself.

Body awareness connects us with our inner world. Awareness of little annoyances, nervousness, or anxiety helps shift perspective and open up to new options other than automatic, habitual reactions. When we pay attention to our bodily sensations, we recognize the ebb and flow of our emotions and can control how we react. Traumatized people, though, are afraid of feeling. To change, it's crucial to focus on sensations and how transient they are. They respond to slight shifts in body position, changes in breathing, and shifts in thinking. Practicing mindfulness calms the sympathetic nervous system, making you less likely to move into fight or flight. Mindfulness has been shown to have a positive effect on numerous stress-related symptoms, including depression and chronic pain. It can also positively affect physical health by improving immune response, blood pressure, and cortisol levels.

BREATHWORK TECHNIQUES FOR TRAUMA RELEASE

Dr. Van Der Kolk presents the science behind how breathing, chanting, and moving can directly train our arousal system. Breathwork is a powerful tool for releasing stored trauma. It connects directly with your autonomic nervous system, which regulates essential bodily functions like heart rate, digestion, and respiratory rate. Engaging in intentional breathwork activates the parasympathetic nervous system, promoting relaxation and reducing stress; in other words, it can put the brakes on the arousal system. This activation helps regulate emotional responses, making breathwork an invaluable trauma-release practice. Breathwork can calm the mind, decrease anxiety, and create a sense of safety in your body. It's a simple yet profound way to access and release deep-seated emotional pain.

One effective technique is the Trauma Release Breath (TRB). To begin, find a quiet, comfortable space where you won't be disturbed. Sit or lie down in a relaxed position. Close your eyes and take a few deep breaths to center yourself. Inhale deeply through your nose for a count of four, allowing your abdomen to rise. Hold your breath for a count of four, then exhale slowly through your mouth for eight, letting your abdomen fall. Repeat this cycle for several minutes, focusing on the sensation of your breath entering and leaving your body. This method helps regulate your nervous system and release stored emotional tension. The more you stay focused on your breathing, the more you will benefit, particularly if you pay attention until the end of the out-breath and then wait a moment before inhaling again.

Another powerful technique is Holotropic breathing, developed by Dr. Stanislav Grof. This method involves rapid, deep breathing to induce an altered state of consciousness, allowing for deep emotional release. To practice Holotropic breathing, lie down comfortably with a trusted friend or practitioner nearby to support you. Begin by breathing deeply and rapidly through your mouth, focusing on the rhythm and intensity of your breath. Continue this pattern for 20-30 minutes, allowing any emotions or sensations to surface without judgment. After the session, take time to rest and reflect on your experience. This technique can bring up intense emotions, so it's essential to approach it with care and support.

Regular breathwork practice offers numerous benefits. For one, it helps manage acute stress. When faced with a stressful situation, taking a few moments to practice deep breathing can instantly calm your mind and body. This immediate relief can prevent stress from escalating and affecting your overall well-being. Incorporating breathwork into your daily routine can also promote long-term emotional balance. Set aside a few minutes each day for a dedicated breathwork session. Whether in the morning to start your day with clarity or in the evening to unwind, consistent practice can help regulate your nervous system and improve your emotional resilience.

Guided breathwork sessions can provide additional support and structure. Various online platforms offer trauma-focused breathwork sessions, making practicing from the comfort of your home easy. Websites like Insight Timer and YouTube have numerous guided breathwork videos tailored for trauma release. These sessions often combine breathwork with soothing music or nature sounds, enhancing the overall experience. Audio guides are also available, offering step-by-step instructions for various breathwork techniques. These resources can be invaluable, especially if you're new to breathwork or prefer guided practice.

Incorporating breathwork into your daily life can be transformative. It's a simple, accessible, and effective way to release stored trauma and promote emotional well-being. Techniques like Trauma Release Breath and Holotropic breathing can regulate your nervous system, manage stress, and create a sense of safety. With regular practice and the support of guided sessions, breathwork can become a powerful tool for healing and self-care.

THERAPEUTIC MOVEMENT FOR EMOTIONAL RELEASE

There's something profoundly liberating about moving your body in natural and expressive ways. Therapeutic movement allows you to connect with and release stored trauma by engaging your body in motion. When you move, you activate various systems in your body that help process and release pent-up emotions. Think of your body as a vessel that holds both your physical self and your emotional experiences. Movement becomes a way to stir and release these emotions, helping you process trauma that words alone might not reach.

One powerful way to unlock stored trauma is through shaking and tremoring exercises. These exercises mimic the natural responses animals have after a stressful event. Animals shake off the stress and move on, but humans often suppress this natural response. To practice this, stand with your feet shoulder-width apart and knees slightly bent. Begin by shaking your hands and arms, then gradually let the shaking spread to your shoulders, torso, legs, and feet. Allow your body to tremble and shake freely without judgment. This simple yet effective exercise can help release tension and trauma stored in your muscles, leaving you feeling lighter and more relaxed.

Dance and expressive movement are other powerful tools for emotional liberation. When you dance, you engage your entire body in a flow of movements that can express a wide range of emotions. You don't need to follow specific steps or routines; the key is to let your body move in ways that feel right for you. Put on your favorite music and let yourself dance freely. Pay attention to how your body feels as you move. Notice any areas of tension or discomfort and allow the movement to help release those feelings. Expressive movement can also include gestures and postures that reflect your inner state. For instance, if you're feeling angry, you might find relief in stomping your feet or making solid and decisive movements with your arms. These actions can help you process and release intense emotions, providing emotional and physical relief.

I was introduced to a movement program called TranscenDANCE™ a few years ago. TranscenDANCE™ is a fun and liberating conscious dance modality for all ages and mobility levels. Created by Jennifer Joy Jiménez of the Brave Thinking Institute, this movement was birthed out of personal development, mind/body/spirit practices, spiritual psychology, somatics, and energy healing. The movement is self-guided, with no steps to follow, as you allow the music, your spirit, and your body to move you from the inside out. The six tools of TranscenDANCE™ include breath, sound, energy, music, movement, and mind. Jiménez calls this transcendent dance, "The secret language of your soul, a healing balm for your body, a pathway for transformation, and a haven for your innermost thoughts, feelings, and dreams to be expressed freely."

Consistent movement practice is crucial for releasing trauma, whether it is dancing, walking, or rhythmic movement like Tai Chi. Regular movement helps you stay connected to your body and know how it holds and processes emotions. It's not just about the immediate release but about building a routine that supports ongoing healing. Enhanced body awareness through movement allows you to tune into your body's signals and respond appropriately. This ongoing practice can help you manage stress more effectively and maintain emotional balance. The physical benefits are significant as well. Regular movement improves circulation, flexibility, and overall physical health, supporting emotional well-being.

Creating a personal movement practice doesn't have to be complicated. Start by setting up a safe space where you can move freely without interruptions. An appropriate space might be a corner of your living room, a quiet spot in your garden, or even a local park. Make sure the space feels comfortable and inviting. You might want to add elements like soft lighting, calming music, or even a few plants to enhance the atmosphere. Once you have your space, think about combining movement with other somatic practices.

For example, you might start your session with a few minutes of breathwork to center yourself, followed by shaking exercises to release tension, and then transition into freeform dance or expressive movement.

One helpful tip is to create a playlist of songs that inspire different moods and movements. Music can make your practice more enjoyable and help you connect with various emotions. You might have a few upbeat songs for energetic dancing, some slower tunes for gentle, flowing movements, and perhaps a few tracks that evoke deeper emotions for more expressive gestures. Experiment with different types of music and movements to find what resonates with you. Remember, there's no right or wrong way to move. The goal is to listen to your body and let it guide you.

Regularly integrating therapeutic movement into your routine can be transformative. It's a way to honor and release stored emotions, helping you move forward with a lighter, more balanced sense of self. Whether you're shaking off stress, dancing with joy, or expressing deep emotions through movement, these practices can provide a powerful path to healing.

SELF-MASSAGE TECHNIQUES FOR TRAUMA RELEASE

The power of touch is profound, especially when it comes to releasing stored trauma. Applying touch to your body sends signals to your nervous system that can help calm and soothe you. Self-massage can become a valuable tool. Engaging in self-massage techniques helps activate your parasympathetic nervous system, which is responsible for rest and relaxation. By doing so, you can alleviate physical symptoms of trauma and create a sense of safety and comfort within your body. The act of touching and massaging yourself can also help release endorphins, your body's natural painkillers, promoting a sense of well-being and relaxation.

One effective self-massage technique is myofascial release. This method focuses on relieving tension in the fascia, the connective tissue that surrounds your muscles. You will need a foam roller or a small, firm ball like a tennis ball to practice myofascial release. Begin by placing the foam roller or ball under the area of tension, such as your back or thighs. Gently roll back and forth, applying pressure to the tight spots. Take your time and breathe deeply as you work through the tension. This technique helps break up adhesions and improve blood flow, reducing pain and enhancing mobility.

Another technique to explore is acupressure, which involves applying pressure to specific points on your body to release emotional and physical tension. Acupressure points, also known as acupoints, are believed to be connected to energy pathways in your body. To practice acupressure for emotional release, find a quiet, comfortable place to sit or lie down. Some commonly used acupoints for emotional release include the "Yintang" point between your eyebrows and the "Pericardium 6" point on the inner forearm, about three finger-widths from the wrist crease. Gently press and hold these points with your fingertips for a few minutes, breathing deeply and focusing on the sensations. This action can help release pent-up emotions and promote a sense of calm.

Incorporating self-massage into your daily routine can benefit your physical and emotional well-being in the long term. Regular self-massage helps reduce physical tension, promote relaxation, and relieve pain. Over time, this practice can improve your body awareness, making it easier to identify and address areas of tension before they escalate. Additionally, self-massage can enhance your emotional well-being by providing a tangible way to practice self-care and self-compassion. Taking the time to nurture and care for your body can foster a deeper connection with yourself, promoting overall well-being.

There are numerous resources available to support your self-massage practice. Books like "The Trigger Point Therapy Workbook" by Clair Davies offer detailed instructions and illustrations for various self-massage techniques. This book is a valuable guide that can help you target specific areas of tension and learn how to release them effectively. Online tutorials are also a great resource, providing visual demonstrations that can make it easier to understand and follow the techniques. Websites like YouTube host countless self-massage videos covering everything from myofascial release to acupressure. These tutorials often include step-by-step instructions and tips to help you get the most out of your practice.

Several apps and online platforms offer guided self-massage sessions for those who prefer guided support. Apps like "Insight Timer" and "Calm" provide audio guides that walk you through various self-massage techniques, making it easy to practice anytime, anywhere. These guided sessions can be beneficial if you are new to self-massage or prefer having structured support. Additionally, some wellness centers and spas offer virtual workshops or classes on self-massage, providing an opportunity to learn from experienced practitioners and connect with others who share your interest in holistic healing.

Engaging in self-massage is a powerful way to support your healing process. Techniques like myofascial release and acupressure can release physical and emotional tension, promoting relaxation and well-being. Regular practice helps alleviate pain and discomfort and fosters a deeper connection with your body. With the support of books, videos, and guided sessions, you can develop a self-massage routine that enhances your overall health and nurtures your emotional resilience.

USING SOUND AND VIBRATION TO AID TRAUMA RELEASE

Sound and vibration are potent tools in trauma therapy. They influence your body's physiological responses, helping release stored trauma and promoting emotional healing. When sound waves travel through your body, they create vibrations that can penetrate deep into your tissues, stimulating relaxation and stress relief. These vibrations can alter your brainwave patterns, encouraging a shift from the beta state (associated with active thinking) to the alpha or theta states (associated with relaxation and meditation). This shift helps calm the nervous system, making it easier to process and release emotional pain.

Traditional and modern sound healing practices offer various ways to harness the power of sound for trauma release. One traditional practice is singing bowls, which have been used for centuries in Tibetan and Himalayan cultures. These bowls produce harmonic sounds and vibrations when struck or played with a mallet. The vibrations resonate throughout your body, promoting a sense of calm and balance. Years ago, a good friend gifted me my first singing bowl on a little cushion. Since then, I have acquired a crystal singing bowl tuned to the heart chakra. Sacred objects like these are significant assets to keep in your sacred healing space.

Modern healing practices include sound baths, where you are immersed in sound waves produced by instruments such as gongs, chimes, and crystal bowls. These sound baths create a meditative state, allowing your mind and body to relax and release tension.

To incorporate sound healing into your trauma release practice, consider using singing bowls for vibrational healing. Start by finding a quiet space where you can sit comfortably. Place the singing bowl on a cushion or hold it in your hand. Gently strike the bowl's rim with a mallet to produce a resonant sound. As the sound fills the room, close your eyes and focus on the vibrations. Allow the sound to wash over you, noticing any sensations or emotions that arise. This practice can help release stored tension and promote a sense of peace.

Chanting and vocal toning exercises are also practical sound healing techniques. Chanting involves repeating specific sounds or mantras to create vibrations within your body. One famous mantra is "Om," which is believed to represent the universal sound of creation. To practice chanting, sit comfortably and take a few deep breaths. Begin by chanting "Om" slowly and steadily, allowing the sound to resonate in your chest and throat. Feel the vibrations and notice how they affect your body and mind. Vocal toning involves using your voice to produce specific tones to help release tension and promote healing. Experiment with different tones and pitches, paying attention to how they feel in your body.

Integrating sound therapy into your daily life can offer significant benefits. Regular, sound healing practices can help calm your nervous system, reduce stress, and promote emotional balance. Consider incorporating sound healing into your daily routine by setting aside a few minutes each day for a sound healing session. Whether playing a singing bowl, chanting a mantra, or listening to soothing music, these practices can help create a sense of calm and relaxation. You might find it helpful to start your day with a short sound healing session to set a positive tone or end your day with one to unwind and prepare for restful sleep.

Numerous resources are available to support your sound therapy practice. Online platforms like YouTube and Insight Timer offer guided sound healing sessions you can follow. These sessions often include a variety of sound healing techniques, from singing bowls to gongs, providing a rich auditory experience. Additionally, there are many recommended audio tracks specifically designed for home practice. These tracks often feature soothing sounds and frequencies that can help promote relaxation and healing. Websites like Spotify and Apple Music host playlists dedicated to sound healing, making it easy to find and access these resources.

Incorporating sound and vibration into your trauma-release practice can be a transformative experience. Techniques like singing bowls and chanting can tap into the healing power of sound to release stored trauma and promote emotional well-being. Regular practice can help calm your nervous system, reduce stress, and create a sense of inner peace. With the support of guided sessions and audio tracks, sound therapy can become a valuable tool in your holistic healing journey.

USING SELF-HEALING TECHNIQUES TO BALANCE YOUR ENERGY

Early in my exposure to holistic healthcare, I discovered the work of "Healing Touch," created by Janet Mentgen, RN, BSN. At the time, I was the director of a hospice program, which was a steppingstone for me out of the traditional Western healthcare model. My first course in Healing Touch changed the trajectory of my life forever. I just knew this was the next step on my path. Healing Touch started as a nursing modality and quickly moved to a program that anyone could master for self-care and to facilitate healing for others. It is a mind/body/spirit approach to wellness that recognizes we are spiritual beings having this physical experience. Our physical body is within our energy body, where pain, discomfort, and emotions are first manifested before being felt in the physical body. The various Healing Touch techniques focus on repatterning and aligning our whole being by balancing the energy field. It's a systematic approach to healing using energy interventions. Healing Touch is a certification program that equips individuals with a non-invasive, holistic way of healing.

Becoming a practitioner of Healing Touch opened the door for me to many other holistic approaches to healing and wellness. As an instructor, I taught this work worldwide to tens of thousands of students. Here is an example of balancing your energy field and energy centers.

Self-Chakra Balance is a basic balancing technique you can do on yourself. You have major energy centers (chakras) at the base or root area, sacral, solar plexus, heart, throat, brow, and crown of the head. You also have minor energy centers at the joints – ankles, knees, hips, wrists, elbows, and shoulders. This technique balances your energy throughout your system.

Begin by sitting in a chair or lay on a bed. Soft music is a help but optional. Use your breath to become centered and grounded. You will begin by balancing the energy in the lower limbs first. You will be holding each position approximately a minute or until the energy you feel in both hands feel about the same. Bring your right leg up and cross it at the knee of your Left leg. Place one hand on the right ankle and one on the right knee. With intention, visualize healing light from your divine source flowing through the top of your head to your heart, then flowing down both arms and activating your hands while resting on your ankle and knee. You intend to make higher energy available to your body as needed. After about a minute, move the lower hand to the knee and the upper hand to the hip and hold it for approximately a minute. Then, put down your leg and do the same for your left leg. Now, you are ready to move up the center of the body.

Hold your lower hand over the root area and your upper hand on the sacral or lower belly. After a minute, move the lower hand to the sacral and the upper hand to the solar plexus at the end of the breastbone. Again, after a minute, move the lower hand to the solar plexus and the upper hand to the heart. At this point, you can include the arms by using your left hand to grasp your right wrist and your right hand to grasp your left wrist. Then, hold both elbows, followed by both shoulders, hugging yourself. From here, move back to the center of the body and place your lower hand on the heart and the upper hand on the throat. Next, move the lower hand to the throat and the upper to the brow. Finally, the lower hand moves to the brow and the upper hand to the crown of the head. Each position is held for one minute.

In this chapter, we've explored how trauma manifests in the body and methods to release it, from breathwork and movement to sound therapy to Healing Touch. These practices offer pathways to emotional balance and physical well-being. Next, we'll explore managing stress and anxiety, providing more tools to enhance your holistic healing journey.

CHAPTER FIVE

MANAGING STRESS AND ANXIETY

As I sat with my friend, Anne, on her porch one evening, we watched as the sun dipped below the horizon. Out of this quiet moment, she confessed that lately, she felt like a pressure cooker ready to explode. The constant demands of work, caring for her aging parents, and the daily grind left her feeling exhausted and anxious. Anne's heart raced frequently, and she often woke up with pounding headaches. She felt trapped in a relentless cycle of stress. If this sounds familiar, you're not alone. Many face similar challenges regarding child-rearing, working, and caring for aging parents. Understanding how stress and anxiety impact your body is the first step toward finding relief.

THE IMPACT OF STRESS AND ANXIETY ON THE BODY

When you experience stress or anxiety, your body immediately reacts with a survival mechanism that dates back to our ancestors. When faced with danger, their bodies needed to respond quickly to either fight or flee. We know this as the fight-flight-or-freeze response. When activated, your body releases stress hormones like cortisol and adrenaline. These hormones increase your heart rate and blood pressure to prepare for immediate action. While this response is beneficial in short bursts, chronic stress keeps your body constantly alert, leading to numerous physical symptoms.

One of the most noticeable effects of chronic stress and anxiety is muscle tension. Your muscles tighten as a natural reflex to protect your body from injury. However, when this tension becomes constant, it can lead to headaches, back pain, and other discomforts. Many people experience tension headaches, which can be debilitating and affect daily life. Additionally, the constant activation of the fight-flight-or-freeze response can lead to digestive issues, as the body diverts energy away from non-essential functions like digestion during periods of stress, resulting in stomachaches, constipation, or diarrhea.

The long-term consequences of chronic stress and anxiety are significant. Persistent high blood pressure, or hypertension, is a common result of prolonged stress. Hypertension increases your risk of heart disease, stroke, and other cardiovascular problems. Chronic stress also weakens your immune system, making you more susceptible to illnesses. You might notice that you catch colds more frequently or take longer to recover from minor ailments. Also, prolonged stress can lead to sleep disturbances, weakening your immune system and exacerbating other health issues.

The stress response is a complex process involving multiple body systems. When you perceive a threat, the hypothalamus in your brain sends signals to the adrenal glands, prompting the release of adrenaline and cortisol. These hormones prepare your body for immediate action by increasing your heart rate, blood pressure, and blood sugar levels. Adrenaline boosts your energy levels, while cortisol helps your body maintain that energy by releasing glucose into your bloodstream. However, cortisol levels remain elevated when stress becomes chronic, leading to various health problems.

While I was working as a young nurse in intensive care in the seventies, I was only in my twenties when I experienced high levels of stress that I was not prepared to handle. We didn't know that much about the long-term effects of stress at that time, so doctors treated my symptoms of painful neck spasms with cortisone injections. When you don't address the causes of the stress, problems will eventually develop in other places. For me, that was migraine headaches and hypertension, for which I was prescribed medications. At the time, I was thoroughly ingrained in the Western healthcare model and saw "alternative solutions" as a waste of money. For many years afterward, a cascade of stress responses ensued before I woke up and embraced a holistic approach to my health. Meditation, massage, chiropractic, and energy healing literally saved my life and opened the door for me to change my work in the world.

Here is another story about a woman in her late fifties who developed hypertension due to chronic work-related stress. Mary worked in a high-pressure environment, often working long hours and dealing with demanding clients. Over time, the constant stress took a toll on her body. She began experiencing frequent headaches, fatigue, and a racing heart. A visit to her doctor revealed that her blood pressure was dangerously high. Realizing the impact of stress on her health, Mary decided to make significant changes. She started practicing relaxation techniques, took regular breaks, and sought professional help to manage her anxiety. Over time, her blood pressure normalized, and she felt more in control of her health. Mary was one of the lucky ones who listened to her body.

Another powerful testimonial comes from Lisa, a reader who struggled with chronic headaches for years. Lisa's headaches were so severe that they affected her ability to work and enjoy her favorite activities. She tried various treatments, but nothing seemed to provide lasting relief. Finally, Lisa decided to address her stress and anxiety head-on. She started incorporating stress management techniques, such as deep breathing exercises and mindfulness practices, into her daily routine. Gradually, her headaches became less frequent and less intense. Lisa's story highlights the importance of managing stress to improve overall well-being.

Reflection Section

Take a moment to reflect on how stress and anxiety manifest in your body. Do you experience headaches, muscle tension, or digestive issues? Write down your observations and consider how chronic stress might affect your overall health. Acknowledging these symptoms is the first step toward finding effective stress management techniques that work for you.

Understanding the physiological effects of stress and anxiety can empower you to take control of your health. By recognizing the signs and addressing the root causes, you can break free from the cycle of stress and build a healthier, more balanced life.

GROUNDING EXERCISES FOR INSTANT STRESS RELIEF

Grounding is a technique that anchors you to the present moment, helping you pull away from distressing thoughts and overwhelming emotions. It's a powerful tool for managing stress and anxiety, especially when you need immediate relief. Grounding lies in reconnecting with your body and the environment around you. This connection helps divert your focus from anxious thoughts to the tangible, grounding you in the here and now. By doing this, grounding exercises can reduce anxiety and panic attacks, offering a sense of calm and control in moments of distress.

One of the most effective grounding techniques is the 5-4-3-2-1 method. This exercise engages your senses to bring you back to the present. Start by taking a deep breath. Then, look around and identify five things you can see. Next, focus on four things you can touch, such as the fabric of your clothes or the texture of a nearby object. Continue listening for three sounds, whether birds chirping outside or the hum of an appliance. Move on to noticing two things you can smell: the scent of your hand lotion or the aroma of a candle. Finally, identify one thing you can taste, like a sip of water or the taste of gum. This technique is simple yet effective in shifting your focus away from stress and grounding you at the moment.

Another grounding exercise involves using sensory awareness. It can be as straightforward as placing your hands in water and concentrating on the temperature and sensation. Alternatively, you could pick up or touch items near you, focusing on their texture, weight, and color. Listening to your surroundings, such as the rustle of leaves or distant traffic, can also help anchor you. These exercises work by engaging your senses, distracting your mind from anxious thoughts, and bringing your attention back to the present.

Tangible objects play a significant role in grounding exercises. Items like a stress ball or worry stone can be incredibly soothing. Holding and squeezing a stress ball can help release built-up tension when you feel overwhelmed. Similarly, a worry stone, a small, smooth stone you can rub between your fingers, can provide a calming tactile sensation. Another option is to focus on a piece of fabric or textured item. Paying attention to the item's texture, warmth, and feel can help ground you and reduce anxiety.

Incorporating grounding exercises into your daily life can be both practical and beneficial. Quick grounding exercises during work breaks help manage stress and maintain focus. For instance, if you're feeling anxious at work, take a five-minute break to practice the 5-4-3-2-1 technique or touch a grounding object like a stress ball. These short breaks can make a significant difference in your overall stress levels. Grounding techniques are also useful for managing specific situations, such as public speaking anxiety. Before speaking, take a moment to ground yourself by focusing on your breath or holding a textured item in your pocket. This action can help calm your nerves and boost your confidence.

Grounding is an accessible and effective way to manage stress and anxiety. By reconnecting with your body and the environment around you, you can anchor yourself in the present moment, reducing anxiety and panic attacks. Whether through sensory awareness, grounding objects, or incorporating these techniques into your daily routine, grounding provides immediate relief and helps build long-term resilience.

MINDFULNESS PRACTICES TO REDUCE ANXIETY

Mindfulness is a powerful practice that can significantly reduce anxiety. But what exactly is mindfulness? At its core, mindfulness means paying attention to the present moment without judgment. It's about being fully aware of where and what you're doing without getting overly reactive or overwhelmed by what's happening around you. This practice helps you break the cycle of stress and anxiety by grounding you in the here and now. Focusing on the present moment creates space to observe your thoughts and feelings without getting caught up in them. Focusing can lead to a greater sense of calm and emotional balance.

One of the simplest and most effective mindfulness exercises is mindful breathing. This practice involves focusing on your breath and observing how it feels as it enters and leaves your body. To start, find a comfortable position, either sitting or lying down. Close your eyes and breathe deeply through your nose, feeling your chest and abdomen rise. Exhale slowly through your mouth, noticing the sensation of the air leaving your body. To increase the power of this breathing, purse your lips as you blow out. Continue to breathe deeply and slowly, paying attention to each inhale and exhale. If your mind wanders, gently bring your focus back to your breath. This exercise can help calm your mind and reduce anxiety, making it easier to manage stressful situations.

Another effective mindfulness practice is the body scan meditation. This exercise helps you become more aware of your physical sensations, which can be particularly helpful for reducing anxiety. To perform a body scan:

1. Find a quiet, comfortable place to sit or lie down without interruptions.
2. Close your eyes and take a few deep breaths to center yourself.
3. Start by focusing on the top of your head, noticing any sensations or tension.
4. Gradually move your attention down to your forehead, eyes, cheeks, jaw, and neck, pausing at each point to observe how it feels.
5. Continue this process, moving down through your shoulders, arms, chest, abdomen, hips, legs, and feet.
6. Spend a few moments on each area, noticing any sensations or tension.

This exercise helps you become more aware of your body and promotes relaxation and stress relief.

Incorporating mindfulness into your daily activities can make a significant difference in managing anxiety. Mindful eating is a great place to start. Instead of rushing through your meals, take the time to savor each bite. Notice the colors, textures, and flavors of your food. Chew slowly and pay attention to how the food feels in your mouth. This practice can help you enjoy your meals more and reduce mindless eating, often driven by stress or boredom. Another way to practice mindfulness is during daily chores, such as washing dishes or folding laundry. Instead of letting your mind wander, focus on the task at hand. Notice the sensation of the water on your hands, the texture of the dishes, or the feel of the fabric as you fold it. These simple practices can help you stay present and reduce anxiety throughout the day.

Numerous mindfulness apps and websites are available for those who prefer guided support. Apps like:

- Headspace
- Calm
- BrainTap
- Innercise

These apps offer guided mindfulness meditation sessions, making incorporating mindfulness into your daily routine effortless. These apps provide a variety of meditation lengths and themes, allowing you to choose the one that best fits your needs. Websites like Mindful.org also offer many resources, including articles, guided meditations, and mindfulness exercises. Online platforms like YouTube host numerous guided mindfulness meditation sessions, offering free access to high-quality guided practices. These resources can be beneficial, especially if you're new to mindfulness or find it challenging to focus on your own.

Mindfulness practices can significantly reduce anxiety and improve overall well-being. Focusing on the present moment and incorporating simple exercises like mindful breathing and body scan meditation into your daily routine can create a greater sense of calm and emotional balance. Whether through conscious eating, daily chores, or guided meditation sessions, mindfulness provides valuable tools for managing anxiety and enhancing your quality of life.

CREATING A STRESS-RELIEF TOOLKIT

Imagine having a personalized collection of tools and techniques at your fingertips, ready to help you manage stress whenever needed. That's what a stress-relief toolkit is all about. It's a carefully curated set of items and practices designed to bring immediate relief and long-term benefits. The beauty of a stress-relief toolkit is its versatility. It can be tailored to your specific needs and preferences, making it a go-to resource for managing stress effectively. Having this toolkit means you don't have to scramble for solutions when stress hits; everything you need is right there, ready to provide comfort and calm.

So, what should you include in your stress-relief toolkit? Start with aromatherapy oils. Essential oils like lavender, chamomile, and eucalyptus are known for their calming properties. You can use them in a diffuser to fill your room with a soothing scent or apply them topically to pulse points for quick relaxation. Another essential item is a stress-relief journal. Writing down your thoughts and feelings can be incredibly therapeutic. It helps you process emotions and gain clarity, making it easier to manage stress. Your journal can also be a place to track your progress and reflect on your journey to better mental health.

Using these items effectively is key to reaping their benefits. For aromatherapy oils, you have a couple of options. Diffusion is a great way to create a calming environment. Add a few drops of your chosen essential oil to a diffuser and let it fill the room with its soothing aroma. For topical application, place a drop or two on your wrists, temples, or behind your ears. Inhale deeply to enjoy the calming effects. Just make sure you are using a 100% pure essential oil and not a cheap imitation. If it didn't cost much, it wasn't pure! I once bought a 10 ml bottle of rose oil. The label said 100% pure in jojoba oil, and I paid $12 for it. Yes, it smelled quite rosey, but it was anything other than pure. A pure 100% 5 ml bottle usually costs around $200. It takes two tons of rose petals picked early in the morning from bushes in a protected valley in Turkey or Bulgaria to produce a quarter cup of oil! Word to the wise, do your research before purchasing any essential oil.

Guided prompts can be incredibly helpful for your stress-relief journal. Start by writing about what's causing your stress. Then, reflect on how your body feels in response to this stress. Finally, jot down any steps you can take to alleviate it. These prompts can guide your writing and help you gain deeper insights into your stress triggers and responses.

Personalization and experimentation are crucial components of an effective stress-relief toolkit. Think about what brings you comfort and joy. Adding personal items, such as a favorite book or calming music, can make your toolkit even more effective. For instance, if you love reading, include a book that uplifts you. If music calms you, create a playlist of your favorite soothing tracks. Experiment with different stress-relief techniques to find what works best for you. You may discover that a five-minute meditation session works wonders, or perhaps you'll find that a quick walk outside instantly lifts your mood. The key is to try various methods and see what resonates with you.

In addition to these items, consider including a few more elements to round out your toolkit. A small, comforting object like a worry stone or a piece of soft fabric can provide immediate tactile relief when you're feeling anxious. Guided meditations or breathing exercises can also be invaluable. Apps like Calm and Innercise® offer a wide range of guided sessions you can access anytime. You should also include a list of positive affirmations. Reading these affirmations can help shift your mindset and reduce stress.

Making your stress-relief toolkit a part of your daily routine can enhance effectiveness. Please keep it where you can easily access it, like your bedside table or a drawer at work. The convenience of having everything in one place means you're more likely to use it regularly, making these tools truly powerful. Over time, you'll find yourself better equipped to handle stress and maintain a sense of calm and balance.

Creating a stress-relief toolkit is a proactive step toward managing stress and enhancing overall well-being. By personalizing it and experimenting with different techniques, you can develop tools that effectively support your mental health. This toolkit becomes a reliable resource, always available to help you navigate the ups and downs of daily life.

INTEGRATING STRESS MANAGEMENT INTO DAILY LIFE

Consistency in stress management is crucial for effective relief. Think of it like brushing your teeth—something you must do daily to maintain good health. Regular practice of stress-relief activities helps keep anxiety at bay and promotes overall well-being. Setting a daily schedule for stress management can make it easier to stick to these practices. Incorporate morning mindfulness meditation to start your day with calm and purpose. This practice could be a simple five-minute session where you focus on your breath and set an intention for the day. Consider relaxation techniques such as deep breathing or a warm bath in the evening to prepare your body and mind for restful sleep.

Building stress management into your daily routines doesn't have to be complicated. Small, consistent actions can make a big difference. For example, consider setting aside ten minutes after lunch to practice a few grounding exercises or take a short walk. These small breaks can help you reset and recharge, making handling the rest of your day easier. Consistency is key, so try to make these activities a regular part of your schedule. Over time, they will become second nature, helping you maintain a balanced and stress-free life.

To help you get started, here's a sample daily stress management routine. Begin your morning with a mindfulness meditation session. Find a quiet spot, sit comfortably, and close your eyes. Focus on your breath, inhaling deeply and exhaling slowly. Spend five to ten minutes in this state, allowing your mind and body to wake up gently. Midday, take a short break for a grounding exercise. The 5-4-3-2-1 technique is perfect for this. In the evening, wind down with some relaxation techniques. Consider a warm bath with essential oils, a few minutes of deep breathing, or listening to calming music. This routine is simple yet effective, helping you manage stress throughout the day.

Maintaining motivation can be challenging, but a few strategies can help. Keeping a stress management journal is an excellent way to track your progress and stay committed. Write down your daily practices, challenges, and how you feel afterward. Writing helps you see your progress and provides insights into what works best. Celebrating milestones is another way to stay motivated. Whether it's a week of consistent practice or a noticeable improvement in your stress levels, take the time to acknowledge and celebrate these achievements. This positive reinforcement can keep you motivated and committed to your stress management practices.

Flexibility and adaptation are also crucial. Life is unpredictable, and there will be days when your usual routine isn't feasible. On busy days, adapt your techniques to fit your available time. If you can't do an entire mindfulness session, take a few deep breaths while waiting in line or practice a quick grounding exercise at your desk. Adapting your routines based on your needs and lifestyle ensures you can maintain stress management practices even when life gets hectic. This flexibility helps you stay consistent, which is essential for long-term success.

Stress management is ongoing, and finding what works best for you is essential. Integrating stress-relief activities into your daily life, maintaining motivation, and adapting your practices can effectively manage stress and improve your overall well-being. This approach helps you cope with stress and enhances your quality of life, making navigating your challenges easier.

You may be wondering at this point whether I ever learned to manage the stress I described in my own life. While none of us are perfect at it, I have become more relaxed and less stressed over the years. I have incorporated many of my recommendations in this book, having tried all of them. Journaling, affirmations, breathing, music, essential oils, meditating, movement, reading, and laughter are part of my daily activities that help me stay balanced. I continue to learn something new every day and attend retreats, pilgrimages, and educational programs that keep my mind sharp and inspired. I subscribe to the belief that each day is a miracle, an opportunity to grow, and each day is a gift!

In this chapter, we've explored various strategies to manage stress and anxiety effectively. Incorporating these practices into daily life can build a strong foundation for long-term emotional and physical well-being. Now, let's move forward to understand how therapeutic movement can further enhance your holistic healing process.

CHAPTER SIX

ESTABLISHING SELF-CARE ROUTINES

When I first met Jack, he was a vibrant 40-year-old who had always been the rock for his family and friends. However, he began to feel the weight of years of caregiving and work-related stress. Jack was one of those men caught in the middle - raising teenagers and caring for his ailing parents who lived with him and his wife. His energy was dwindling, and he often felt disconnected from his own needs. One day, during a casual conversation, he told me he was running on empty. This revelation wasn't unique to Jack; many men and women find themselves in similar situations where they prioritize everyone else's needs over their own. The power of self-care has much to offer in these kinds of situations. Here are some ideas that may help you if you are one of those who always thinks of everyone else rather than yourself.

THE ROLE OF SELF-CARE IN SOMATIC THERAPY

Self-care is not just a trendy term - you probably have been practicing some form of self-care most of your life but have yet to identify it as such. It's a vital component of the healing process, especially in Somatic Therapy. When you take care of yourself you are creating a balance between your mind and body and thus supporting your somatic therapy goals. I liken it to how you prepare fertile soil before planting seeds; without it, the seeds may struggle to grow. Engaging in regular self-care helps you maintain the emotional resilience needed to navigate life's challenges. It acts as a buffer against burnout, ensuring you have the energy and emotional capacity to face stressors without feeling overwhelmed.

Regular self-care practices prevent burnout by offering consistent opportunities to recharge and rejuvenate. Self-care is all those little, daily acts that keep your emotional and physical well-being in check. These practices can range from taking a few minutes each day to meditate to engaging in a hobby that brings you joy. Incorporating self-care into your routine creates a sustainable way to manage stress and maintain overall health. It's about making self-care a non-negotiable part of your life, like brushing your teeth or having a meal.

Self-care enhances body awareness, a crucial aspect of Somatic Therapy. When you engage in self-care activities, you're tuning into your physical sensations and becoming more attuned to your body's needs. For example, practices like mindful eating help you pay attention to how different foods make you feel, fostering a deeper connection with your body. Similarly, doing a few gentle stretches, yoga or Tai Chi can help you identify and release areas of tension. Doing these activities tunes you to your physical sensations, making it easier to recognize when your body is signaling for rest, nourishment, or movement.

Various forms of self-care contribute to this enhanced body awareness. Physical self-care includes activities like regular exercise and proper nutrition. Exercise doesn't have to be strenuous; even a daily walk or a gentle yoga session can make a significant difference. Proper nutrition involves consuming a balanced diet rich in vitamins, minerals, fresh fruits, vegetables, whole grains, lean proteins, and healthy fats. These practices keep your body healthy and improve your mood and energy levels. Emotional self-care, on the other hand, includes activities like journaling and talk therapy. Writing down your thoughts and feelings can provide clarity and help you process emotions. Talk therapy provides a safe space to explore and address deeper emotional issues, enhancing your emotional resilience.

Take, for instance, the story of Beth, a woman in her early sixties who struggled with chronic stress and anxiety. She incorporated self-care practices into her daily routine, starting with a few minutes of journaling each morning. Over time, she noticed a significant improvement in her emotional health. Writing down her thoughts helped her gain perspective and manage her stress more effectively. Beth's testimonial highlights how simple self-care practices can profoundly impact emotional well-being.

Another example is Christine, who faced constant fatigue and low energy due to her demanding job and family responsibilities. She prioritized self-care by incorporating regular exercise and mindful eating into her routine. Christine started with short, daily walks and gradually added more physical activities as her energy levels improved. She also paid closer attention to her diet, choosing nutrient-rich foods that supported her overall health. Over time, Christine noticed a remarkable reduction in her stress levels and an increase in her energy and vitality. Her case study demonstrates how consistent self-care can reduce stress and improve physical health, providing the resilience needed to handle daily challenges.

Reflection Section

Take a moment to reflect on your current self-care practices. Are there areas where you could use more attention? Write down one or two self-care activities you can incorporate into your routine this week. Notice how these practices affect your overall well-being and sense of connection to your body.

By prioritizing self-care, you support the goals of Somatic Therapy and create a solid foundation for healing. Regular self-care practices enhance body awareness, prevent burnout, and build emotional resilience, making navigating life's ups and downs easier. Whether through physical activities, emotional support, or a combination, self-care is essential for maintaining overall health and well-being.

DESIGNING A PERSONALIZED SELF-CARE PLAN

You might wonder where to start when it comes to self-care. The first step is to assess your needs. Think about areas in your life that require more attention. Reflective exercises can help with this. Find a quiet spot, grab a journal, and ask yourself some key questions: What activities refresh me? When do I feel most drained? How often do I prioritize my needs? Write down your answers without judgment. These reflections will highlight the areas in your life that need more care. You may notice you rarely take time for yourself or that your diet could improve. Identifying these areas is the foundation for your self-care plan.

Setting realistic and achievable goals is crucial for success. You don't want to overwhelm yourself with too many changes at once. Instead, use the SMART criteria: Specific, Measurable, Achievable, Relevant, and Time-bound. For example, if you want to exercise more, a SMART goal might be: "I will walk for 30 minutes, three times a week, for the next month." This goal is specific (walking), measurable (30 minutes), achievable (three times a week), relevant (improves physical health), and time-bound (one month). Another example could be: "I will write in my journal for 10 minutes every evening for the next two weeks." These goals are practical and set you up for success.

Creating a detailed plan for your self-care routine can make incorporating these activities into your daily life easier. Start by listing daily and weekly self-care activities. For instance, your daily activities include morning stretches, a healthy breakfast, and evening journaling. Weekly activities could involve a more extended yoga session, a nature walk, or a catch-up call with a friend. Write these activities down in a planner or calendar to remind yourself. Next, create a self-care schedule that fits into your daily life. If mornings are busy, your self-care time is in the evening. The key is to find a routine that works for you and stick to it.

Regularly reviewing and adjusting your self-care plan is essential to ensure it continues to meet your needs. Life is dynamic, and so are your self-care requirements. Set aside time each week to reflect on your self-care activities. Use journaling prompts to guide your reflection: What worked well this week? What didn't? How did these activities make me feel? Write down your thoughts and be honest with yourself. If certain activities aren't as beneficial as you hoped, don't be afraid to adjust your plan. You may need more physical activity or less screen time. The goal is to create a self-care routine that evolves with you and supports your well-being.

Reflection Section

Take a moment to assess your current self-care practices. What areas of your life need more attention? Write down one or two self-care activities you can incorporate into your routine this week. Notice how these practices affect your overall well-being and sense of connection to your body.

Incorporating these steps into your routine can help you create a personalized self-care plan that supports your physical and emotional health. Whether setting realistic goals, creating a detailed plan, or regularly reviewing your progress, these practices can make self-care an integral part of your life. By prioritizing your needs, you can enhance your well-being and navigate life's challenges with greater resilience and ease.

CREATING A MORNING RITUAL TO BALANCE YOUR DAY

Starting your day with intentional morning rituals can set a positive tone, helping you navigate the hours ahead with increased energy and focus. When you wake up and immediately engage in practices that nourish your body and mind, you create a foundation of calm and clarity that can carry you through the day. Imagine beginning each morning with activities that invigorate your senses and center your thoughts. A morning routine can significantly reduce stress and anxiety, making it easier to handle whatever challenges come your way. Morning rituals provide structure and predictability, which can be incredibly grounding.

Simple morning rituals can make a huge difference in how your day unfolds. Consider starting with gentle stretches or yoga. You don't need to commit to a long session; even five to ten minutes can be beneficial. Begin with a few stretches that target areas where tension typically accumulates, like your neck, shoulders, and back. A short yoga sequence can also work wonders. For example, a few rounds of Sun Salutations can help wake up your body and get your blood flowing. This gentle movement prepares your body for the day and helps clear your mind.

Incorporating breathwork and meditation into your morning routine can further enhance your sense of calm and focus. Try beginning your day with a few minutes of deep, mindful breathing. Sit comfortably, close your eyes, and take slow, deep breaths, focusing on the sensation of the air entering and leaving your body. Follow this with a guided meditation to set your intentions for the day. Many apps and online resources offer short, guided meditations specifically designed for the morning. These practices can help you start your day with a clear mind and a peaceful heart. I particularly love the meditations in Innercise™ created by John Assaraf.

Consistency is crucial when it comes to morning rituals. The benefits of these practices are cumulative; the more regularly you engage in them, the more effective they become. Set a consistent wake-up time that allows you enough space to carry out your morning routine without feeling rushed. Creating a morning routine checklist can be helpful. List the activities you want to include, such as stretching, breathwork, and meditation. This checklist can gently remind you of your commitment to self-care, ensuring you start each day with intention and focus.

Effective morning rituals can vary depending on your preferences and lifestyle. One example is a 10-minute yoga sequence designed to boost your energy. Begin with a few rounds of Cat-Cow to wake up your spine, followed by a gentle Downward Dog to stretch your legs and back. Move into a few standing poses like Warrior I and II to build strength and focus. Finish with a seated Forward Fold to calm your mind and prepare for the day ahead.

Another example is a guided morning meditation for clarity and focus. Sit comfortably, close your eyes, and listen to a guided meditation that helps you set your intentions and visualize a positive day. This practice can help you start your day with a clear mind and a peaceful heart.

Imagine the impact of starting each day with these simple yet powerful practices. They prepare your body and mind for the day ahead and create a sense of calm and focus that can help you navigate the challenges of daily life with greater ease. Whether you choose to incorporate stretching, breathwork, meditation, or a combination of these practices, the key is to find what works best for you and make it a consistent part of your morning routine. By doing so, you set a positive tone for the day, helping you approach each moment with clarity, energy, and a sense of peace.

You may wonder what I do for my morning routine. I have several routines, which vary depending on how busy my coming day will be. Before getting out of bed, I reflect on at least three things I'm grateful for. Gratitude helps set my mood for the day. After my morning bathroom ritual, I make a cup of decaffeinated black tea and either go to our screened-in porch to listen to the birds and the nearby traffic and remind myself that these sounds are of life happening all around me or when it is too cool outside, I sit in our living room to watch the light return for another day. After a quick breakfast and shower, I go upstairs to my office, where I have my meditation chair next to the window. I may sit quietly for a 20-30-minute meditation or listen to a guided meditation on Innercise™ or BrainTap. Journaling then completes my preparation for my day, where I remind myself of my vision for the life I love.

CREATING EVENING ROUTINES FOR RESTORATIVE SLEEP

Evening self-care is crucial for ensuring restorative sleep. How you unwind in the evening can set the stage for a deep, restful sleep, which is essential for maintaining your overall well-being. When you engage in evening rituals that promote relaxation, you're signaling to your body that it's time to wind down and prepare for rest. This connection between evening relaxation and better sleep is well-documented.

Establishing a calming routine can help regulate your sleep-wake cycle, making it easier to fall asleep and stay asleep throughout the night. These rituals create a buffer between the stresses of the day and your time of rest, allowing your mind and body to transition smoothly into sleep mode. Incorporating calming evening activities into your routine can significantly enhance the quality of your sleep. Gentle stretching or yoga before bed can help release any tension accumulated in your muscles throughout the day. Consider dedicating a few minutes to a simple stretching routine, focusing on your neck, shoulders, and lower back areas. Poses such as Child's Pose, Legs-Up-The-Wall, and Reclining Bound Angle Pose can be particularly soothing. These gentle movements can help relax your body and calm your mind, making it easier to drift off to sleep. Aromatherapy with calming essential oils is another effective way to prepare for rest. Scents like lavender, chamomile, and sandalwood are known for their relaxing properties. You can use a diffuser to fill your bedroom with these calming aromas or apply a few drops of essential oil to your pillow or wrists—one caution about using lavender for a restful sleep. Less is more! Most people think ten drops must be better if 1-2 drops are good! Right? Wrong! If you use too much lavender at bedtime, it will keep you awake!

Techniques for unwinding and reducing stress are vital components of an effective evening routine. Guided relaxation exercises can help you let go of the day's stress and promote a sense of tranquility. Find a quiet space, close your eyes, and follow a guided relaxation session. This might involve deep breathing exercises, progressive muscle relaxation, or visualization techniques. These practices can help slow your heart rate and quiet your mind, preparing you for restful sleep. Journaling is another powerful tool for processing thoughts and emotions before bed. Spend a few minutes writing down any lingering worries or reflections from the day. This practice can help clear your mind and prevent racing thoughts from waking you.

To illustrate, let's explore some effective evening routines. One example is a bedtime routine with a warm bath and reading a favorite book. Start by warm bathing to relax your muscles and soothe your mind. Add some Epsom salts and 8-10 drops of lavender essential oil to a normal-sized bathtub or 30 drops to a soaking tub to enhance the calming effect. After your bath, spend 20-30 minutes reading a book you enjoy. Choose something light and uplifting, avoiding anything too stimulating or emotionally intense. Combining a warm bath and quiet reading can create a sense of calm and relaxation, making it easier to transition into sleep.

Another example is a guided evening meditation for deep sleep. Find a comfortable position in your bed, close your eyes, and listen to a guided meditation designed to promote deep sleep. Many apps and online platforms offer guided meditations specifically for bedtime. My favorite apps for this are BrainTap and Innercise™. These sessions often include soothing music, gentle guidance, and visualization techniques to help you relieve the day's stress and drift into a peaceful sleep. The key is to choose a meditation that resonates with you and make it a regular part of your evening routine.

My personal routine starts with my Gratitude Journal. I record five things I am grateful for that occurred in my day. It's a great way to reflect on what went well and what I need to forgive or let go of simply. Then I look to my essential oils. I may use several oils specific to any discomfort I may be experiencing, like a painful foot, an achy knee, or a GI upset. Then I apply a drop of lavender to the sole of each foot for restfulness, followed by brushing White Angelica™, a Young Living Blend, through my energy field. White Angelica™ is a protective blend for one's energy field. After this, I climb into bed with an inspirational book and read for 10-20 minutes before turning out the light.

Reflection Section

Take a moment to think about your current evening routine. Are there activities that help you relax and prepare for sleep? Write down one or two calming evening activities you can incorporate into your routine this week. Notice how these practices affect your sleep quality and overall sense of well-being.

Evening routines play a significant role in ensuring restorative sleep. By incorporating calming activities, guided relaxation exercises, and soothing rituals, you can create an environment that supports deep, restful sleep. Whether it's gentle stretching, aromatherapy, or quiet reading, finding what works best for you can make a world of difference in how you feel when you wake up each morning.

INCORPORATING NATURE INTO YOUR SELF-CARE ROUTINE

Spending time in nature can profoundly impact your emotional and physical well-being. Moving to Florida, near the coast, showed me that the beach is not my sacred place. I'm more of a mountain girl who thrives on the clean, clear air and the altitude. Where is your sacred space? The beach or the woods? The outdoors offers a natural sanctuary where you can escape the stresses of daily life and reconnect with yourself. Research shows that being in nature reduces anxiety and improves mood. The fresh air, the sounds of birds chirping, and the sight of green leaves rustling in the wind can lift your spirits and calm your mind. Nature inherently promotes relaxation, making letting go of tension and finding peace easier. When you immerse yourself in the natural world, your body responds positively, enhancing your overall well-being.

Integrating nature into your self-care routine can be done without grand gestures or extensive planning. Simple activities can make a significant difference. Consider taking a daily walk in a nearby park or hiking trail. These outdoor walks provide physical exercise and allow you to breathe fresh air and enjoy the beauty around you. If you have access to a garden, spending time tending to plants can be incredibly therapeutic. Gardening allows you to connect with the earth, fostering a sense of accomplishment and tranquility. Even spending time on your balcony or in your backyard can offer a refreshing change of scenery and a moment to unwind. One of the things my husband and I love to do in good weather is eat our lunch outside in nature, where we can see the trees, watch the birds at the feeders, and admire our flowers. It's a time to relax, share our morning experiences, and discuss our plans for our afternoons.

To deepen your connection with nature, practice mindful walking and sensory awareness during outdoor activities. As you walk, focus on the sensations in your body—how your feet feel against the ground, the movement of your muscles, and the rhythm of your breath. Pay attention to the sights, sounds, and smells around you. Notice the colors of the flowers, the rustling of leaves, and the scent of pine or fresh grass. This mindful approach enhances your experience, allowing you to fully engage with the natural world and cultivate a sense of presence. Nature-focused meditation and grounding exercises can also be beneficial. Find a quiet spot, sit comfortably, and close your eyes. Imagine roots extending from your body into the earth, grounding you and providing stability. Visualize the world's energy flowing through you, bringing a sense of calm and balance.

Or, if you are a beach person, feel the hardness or softness of the sand beneath your feet as you walk along the shore. Feel the wind in your hair and the sun on your body, and listen to the sound of the waves as they crash along the edge. Imagine the life-giving waters connecting you to Source as you now stand at the edge, the water lapping over your feet. Calmness and assurity now permeate your whole being.

There are many ways to weave nature-based self-care activities into your daily routine. For instance, start your day with a morning walk in the park. This simple act can help you wake up your senses and prepare for the day ahead. As you walk, pay attention to your surroundings and take in the beauty of nature. Another idea is to use gardening as a form of mindful movement and relaxation. Spend time tending to your plants, feeling the soil between your fingers, and observing the growth of your garden. This activity connects you with nature and provides a sense of accomplishment and peace.

Incorporating nature into your self-care routine can have lasting benefits for your emotional and physical health. Whether it's through outdoor walks, gardening, or mindful nature practices, these activities can help reduce stress, improve mood, and enhance body awareness. Making nature a regular part of your self-care creates opportunities to relax, recharge, and reconnect with yourself meaningfully.

MAKE A DIFFERENCE WITH YOUR REVIEW
SHARE THE GIFT OF HEALING

"*The best way to find yourself is to lose yourself in the service of others.*"

MAHATMA GANDHI

Helping others can be one of the most rewarding things we do. I've written *Somatic Therapy Simplified* to make holistic healing easy and accessible for everyone, especially for those in the second half of life who want to find balance and comfort in their lives.

Now, I'm asking for your help. Would you take a moment to share your thoughts and leave a review?

Your review doesn't just help me—it helps other people who are curious about somatic therapy but don't know where to begin. Most people look at reviews before choosing a book, and your words could inspire someone to start their own healing journey.

It takes just a minute, but your review can make a big difference. You could help…

- One more person discover the power of somatic therapy.
- One more woman prioritize her own well-being.
- One more reader find relief from stress and emotional imbalance.

To leave your review, scan the QR code or visit the website where you purchased the book. Your review might be exactly what someone needs to make their own life easier, healthier, and more balanced.

Thank you so much for being part of this journey with me. Your support means the world!

With gratitude,

Linda Lee Smith

CHAPTER SEVEN

ENHANCING EMOTIONAL RESILIENCE

I met Alex at a church potluck. Alex had faced many challenges over the years, from losing a loved one to a demanding career that left her feeling drained. She told me she had always felt like she was "getting by," never really thriving. This is where her story gets fascinating. One day, Alex decided to take a different approach. She started exploring ways to enhance her emotional resilience, transforming her life. The story she shared with me is a testament to the power of resilience and the potential we all have to bounce back from adversity. In this chapter I'll explain how.

UNDERSTANDING EMOTIONAL RESILIENCE

Gregg Braden's book Resilience from the Heart states that emotional resilience is the ability to recover quickly from difficulties and adapt to life's challenges. He says it's like having an internal spring that helps you bounce back when life knocks you down. This resilience is crucial for overall well-being, contributing to mental health and emotional stability. When you're emotionally resilient, you can manage stress more effectively, maintain a positive outlook, and navigate life's ups and downs without feeling overwhelmed. Personal resilience makes room for more significant shifts in our lives, especially when extremes are happening in our world. Braden puts forth the idea that when the heart and the brain are "on the same wavelength," there is a coherence generated that creates harmony in the body, preparing us to be our best for whatever we are facing.

Braden goes on to say that when we find the emotions that create greater coherence, we also create greater resilience. He has worked closely with the Institute of Heart Math, which developed what they refer to as "Attitude Breathing," where the heart automatically harmonizes the energy between the heart, mind, and body, increasing coherence and clarity. Attitude Breathing (Heart Coherent Meditation) is about breathing in a replacement attitude for a negative feeling or attitude. For example, say you are feeling stressed, anxious, overwhelmed, sad, or depressed and want to replace that with a more positive feeling or attitude like calmness, balance, ease and peace, appreciation and nonjudgment, and compassion.

Sit in a comfortable position with your feet flat on the floor and set the intention to "take the significance out." Start by breathing in calmness and balance; breathe out stress. Repeat three times. Breathe in ease and peace; breathe out overwhelm. Repeat three times. Breathe in appreciation and nonjudgment; breathe out sadness or depression. Repeat three times. Breathe in compassion and nonjudgement; breathe out guilt. Repeat three times. If you would like voice guidance for this kind of breathing meditation, I have found variations of this Attitude Breathing in Innercise™, created by John Assaraf.

Several factors influence emotional resilience. Genetic predispositions and personality traits play a role, as some people are naturally more resilient than others. However, environmental factors such as support systems and life experiences are also significant. For instance, growing up in a supportive family or having strong friendships can bolster your resilience. On the other hand, facing continuous stress or trauma without adequate support can weaken it. Life experiences, both positive and negative, shape your resilience. Overcoming challenges and learning from failures can enhance it, while unaddressed trauma or chronic stress can diminish it.

Strong emotional resilience has profound benefits, including improved stress management and coping skills. When you're resilient, you can handle stressful situations without becoming overwhelmed. This ability to manage stress effectively leads to greater overall life satisfaction and happiness. Resilient individuals tend to have a more positive outlook on life, better relationships, and a greater sense of purpose. They can navigate life's challenges gracefully and maintain emotional balance even in difficult times.

Let's look at some real-life examples to illustrate the power of emotional resilience. Take the case of John, a man who faced significant life challenges, including a personal severe illness that resulted in the loss of his job. Despite these hardships, John managed to rebuild his life. He sought support from friends, practiced mindfulness, and focused on self-care with the support of his life coach. Within a year, John recovered and began to thrive. He found a new career that he loved and built a solid support network of friends and co-workers. His story shows how resilience can help you overcome even the most daunting obstacles.

Another example is Irene, a reader who shared her testimonial with me. Irene had been struggling with anxiety and depression for years. She felt stuck, unable to move forward. Then, she discovered Somatic Therapy and began to practice techniques that enhanced her emotional resilience. Through regular breathwork, mindfulness, and grounding exercises, Irene significantly improved her emotional well-being. She felt more in control of her emotions, better equipped to handle stress, and more optimistic about the future. Irene's experience highlights how building resilience through somatic practices can lead to profound and lasting changes.

Emotional resilience is not a fixed trait; you can cultivate and strengthen it over time. By understanding what influences resilience and its benefits, you can take steps to enhance your resilience. Whether through building strong support networks, practicing mindfulness, or engaging in self-care, you have the power to become more resilient and thrive amidst life's challenges.

TECHNIQUES TO STRENGTHEN EMOTIONAL RESILIENCE

Mindfulness practices are invaluable tools for enhancing emotional resilience. One of the simplest yet most effective techniques is mindful breathing. This practice involves focusing on your breath to anchor yourself in the present moment. Find a quiet spot, sit comfortably, and close your eyes. Take a deep breath through your nose, allowing your abdomen to rise, and then exhale slowly through your mouth as if breathing through a straw. Repeat this process, paying close attention to the sensation of the breath entering and leaving your body. Mindful breathing helps ground you, reducing anxiety and stress while fostering a sense of calm. Another powerful technique is body scan meditation, which involves mentally scanning your body from head to toe, noting any areas of tension or discomfort. This practice not only helps in emotional regulation but also strengthens your connection with your body, making it easier to identify and address physical manifestations of stress.

Cognitive restructuring is another essential technique for building resilience. This method involves identifying and challenging negative thought patterns that can undermine your emotional stability. Start by paying attention to your inner dialogue, especially during stressful situations. When you notice a negative thought, ask yourself whether it's based on facts or assumptions. Challenge these thoughts by questioning their validity and considering alternative perspectives. For instance, if you catch yourself thinking, "I always mess things up," challenge this by recalling instances where you succeeded. Reframing these thoughts fosters positivity and resilience, helping you view challenges as opportunities for growth rather than insurmountable obstacles.

Self-compassion plays a crucial role in building emotional resilience. It involves treating yourself with the same kindness and understanding you would offer a friend. Self-compassion meditation is a practical exercise to cultivate this mindset. Find a quiet space and sit comfortably. Close your eyes and take a few deep breaths. Imagine a situation where you felt inadequate or failed at something. Instead of criticizing yourself, bring to mind words of kindness and understanding. Repeat phrases like, "May I be kind to myself," or "I am doing the best I can." Daily affirmations can also reinforce self-kindness. Write down positive statements about yourself and repeat them every morning. Over time, these practices can reshape your internal dialogue, making you more resilient to life's challenges.

There are several actionable strategies you can adopt to strengthen your emotional resilience. Developing a gratitude practice is a simple yet powerful method. Each day, take a few minutes to write down three things you're grateful for in your gratitude journal. These can be as simple as a warm cup of tea or a kind gesture from a friend. Focusing on gratitude shifts your attention from what's lacking to what's abundant in your life, fostering a positive mindset. Another effective strategy is setting and achieving small, manageable goals. Break down your larger objectives into smaller tasks and tackle them individually. Each small victory builds confidence and resilience, reinforcing your ability to handle more significant challenges.

Incorporating these techniques into your daily life can substantially impact your emotional resilience. Mindful breathing and body scan meditation help ground and regulate your emotions, while cognitive restructuring challenges negative thoughts and fosters positivity. Self-compassion practices cultivate kindness and understanding towards yourself, building a solid foundation for resilience. Meanwhile, gratitude practices and setting small, achievable goals provide a practical framework for maintaining a positive outlook and managing stress. By integrating these strategies, you can enhance your emotional resilience, navigate life's challenges more effectively, and build a more fulfilling and balanced life.

MANAGING OVERWHELMING EMOTIONS

Overwhelming emotions can feel like an unexpected tidal wave crashing over you when you least expect it. These intense feelings often stem from past trauma or ongoing stress that hasn't been fully resolved. When you experience trauma, your body and mind create protective mechanisms to cope with the immediate threat. However, these mechanisms can become maladaptive over time, leading to heightened emotional responses to even minor stressors. The nervous system plays a crucial role in this process. It regulates your body's response to danger through the sympathetic and parasympathetic systems. When these systems are out of balance, your ability to manage emotions effectively diminishes, making it easier to feel overwhelmed.

Grounding exercises offer immediate relief when emotions become too intense. These simple techniques help anchor you in the present moment, diverting your focus from distressing thoughts and feelings. One effective method is the 5-4-3-2-1 technique, which involves identifying five things you can see, four things you can touch, three things you can hear, two things you can smell, and one thing you can taste. This sensory exercise shifts your attention away from overwhelming emotions and helps you regain control. Another grounding exercise involves physical movement—such as stomping your feet or holding a textured object—to create a tangible connection to the present moment.

Breathwork techniques are equally valuable for calming the nervous system and managing intense emotions. Deep, diaphragmatic breathing activates the parasympathetic nervous system, promoting relaxation and reducing the physiological symptoms of stress. Sit comfortably, close your eyes, and place one hand on your chest and the other on your abdomen. Inhale deeply through your nose, allowing your abdomen to rise more than your chest. Exhale slowly through your mouth, feeling your abdomen fall. Repeat this process several times until you notice a sense of calm. The 4-7-8 breathing technique is another effective option. Inhale through your nose for a count of four, hold your breath for seven counts, and exhale through your mouth for eight counts. This technique can be particularly helpful in moments of acute stress or panic.

Expressing your emotions in a healthy way is vital for emotional regulation. Bottling up feelings can lead to physical and emotional distress, while allowing yourself to express them can provide relief and clarity. Verbalizing your emotions is one effective method. Find a trusted friend, family member, or therapist to talk to about what you're experiencing. Sometimes, just naming your emotions out loud can lessen their intensity. Consider creative outlets such as art or music if verbal expression feels challenging. Drawing, painting, or doodling can provide a non-verbal way to process and express complex emotions. Music can also be a powerful tool; playing an instrument, singing, or simply listening to music that resonates with your feelings can offer a sense of release and connection.

Seeking support is crucial when managing overwhelming emotions. You don't have to navigate these intense feelings alone. Finding a therapist, counselor or coach who specializes in Somatic Therapy can provide you with professional guidance and tailored techniques to manage your emotions. Therapists can offer a safe space to explore your feelings and find effective strategies for emotional regulation. Support groups also offer a sense of community and shared experience. Joining a group where others understand what you're going through can reduce feelings of isolation and provide practical advice. Whether you choose in-person meetings or online forums, these groups can offer valuable support and encouragement.

Incorporating these techniques and seeking support can significantly improve your ability to manage overwhelming emotions. Grounding exercises and breathwork provide immediate relief, while expressing emotions through verbal or creative outlets offers long-term benefits. Professional help and support groups add another layer of support, ensuring you have the resources and community needed to navigate emotional challenges.

THE HEALING POWER OF JOURNALING

Journaling is a powerful tool for emotional healing that offers a way to process emotions and build resilience. It allows you to express your thoughts and feelings freely, providing a therapeutic outlet for emotions that might remain bottled up. Writing helps you gain clarity and insight into your experiences, making understanding and navigating your emotional landscape easier. Putting pen to paper creates a space to reflect on your feelings, identify patterns, and explore solutions. This expressive writing can be incredibly liberating, offering relief and a clearer perspective on life's challenges.

You can explore various journaling practices, each serving different purposes and offering unique benefits. Stream-of-consciousness writing is one such technique. This involves writing continuously without worrying about grammar, punctuation, or the coherence of your thoughts. The goal is to let your thoughts flow freely, capturing whatever comes to mind. This practice can help you uncover hidden emotions and gain insights into your subconscious mind. Another effective method is gratitude journaling, which focuses on fostering positivity. Each day, jot down a few things you are grateful for. These can be simple joys like a warm cup of tea or significant events like a meaningful conversation. Gratitude journaling shifts your focus from what is lacking to what is abundant, cultivating a positive mindset. Reflective journaling, on the other hand, involves processing daily experiences. At the end of each day, take a few minutes to write about your experiences, emotions, and any lessons learned. This practice encourages self-awareness and helps you make sense of your daily interactions and feelings.

To get the most out of your journaling sessions, it can be helpful to use specific prompts and exercises. These prompts guide your writing, helping you explore your emotions and set intentions. For instance, you might start with a prompt like, "What emotions am I feeling right now, and why?" This writing style encourages you to delve into your emotional state and identify underlying causes. Another helpful exercise is setting intentions and goals. Begin by writing down your intentions for the day or week. For example, "I intend to approach challenges with patience and understanding." Setting clear intentions helps you focus your energy and actions towards positive outcomes. Other prompts might include, "Describe a recent event that had a significant impact on you," or "Write about a time when you felt truly happy and content." These exercises help you reflect on your experiences, gain insights, and foster a deeper understanding of yourself.

A mentor of mine taught me about a powerful journaling technique called "The Pruning Shears of Revision" by Neville Goddard, which I would like to share with you. In the evening, with your journal in hand at bedtime, think back on your day as if you were watching a newsreel. If you note a place where you weren't at your best - like cutting someone off in traffic, answering someone in a sharp tone, or maybe even yelling at your kids - take the pruning shears of revision and cut out that part of the tape and replace it with a new piece of tape on how you wish you had responded more lovingly.

Now, this, of course, does not erase your behavior, but what it does is, without judgment, correct in your mind how you desire to be in life. Repeating this action every night will bring more harmony into your life. As for the journal, write down the action and the revision. Over time, this will get easier and change how you are in the world.

The benefits of journaling are well-documented, and many individuals have shared their success stories. Take the case of Mimi, who used journaling to overcome grief after losing her partner. Initially, Mimi found it difficult to talk about her feelings, but writing provided a safe space to express her emotions. Each day, she wrote about her memories, her pain, and her hopes for the future. Over time, Mimi noticed a shift in her emotional state. She felt less burdened by her grief and more connected to her inner strength. Journaling became a therapeutic ritual that helped her navigate the complexities of loss and find a path toward healing. Another testimonial comes from Lynn, a reader who built resilience through consistent journaling. Lynn had been struggling with anxiety and self-doubt. She started a daily journaling practice, focusing on gratitude and reflective writing. As she consistently documented her thoughts and feelings, Lynn began to notice patterns in her anxiety triggers and developed strategies to manage them. Her journal became a tool for self-discovery and emotional regulation, helping her build resilience and confidence.

Journaling offers a versatile and accessible way to enhance emotional resilience and process your emotions. Whether you choose stream-of-consciousness writing, gratitude journaling, or reflective journaling, the key is to write regularly and honestly. Use prompts to guide your sessions and explore techniques to find what resonates with you. Through the simple act of writing, you can gain clarity, foster positivity, and build a stronger, more resilient self.

DEVELOPING A RESILIENCE-BUILDING ROUTINE

Creating a resilience-building routine is like planting a garden. You need regular care and attention to see growth. Consistency is key. Regular practice helps embed these habits into your daily life, making them second nature. Establishing a daily schedule dedicated to resilience practices ensures you give yourself the time and space to nurture your emotional strength. Start by setting aside specific times each day for these activities. This could be as simple as dedicating ten minutes each morning to mindfulness or penciling in reflective journaling like the pruning shears of revision before bed. The goal is to make these practices a regular part of your daily routine, like brushing your teeth or having morning coffee.

Incorporating resilience-building activities into your daily life doesn't have to be complicated. Begin your day with a mindfulness practice. When you wake up, take a few moments to focus on your breath, grounding yourself before the day begins. Follow this with a gratitude practice. Write down three things you're grateful for, no matter how small. Gratitude shifts your mindset and sets a positive tone for the day. In the evening, spend some time journaling. Reflect on your day, jot down any emotions you experienced, and set intentions for the next day. Finish with a relaxation technique, such as deep breathing or a gentle stretch. This evening routine helps you unwind and prepares your mind and body for restful sleep.

Maintaining motivation in your resilience-building routine can be challenging, especially on tough days. Keeping a progress journal can be incredibly helpful. Document your daily practices and any changes in your emotional state. This tracks your progress and serves as a reminder of how far you've come. Setting reminders can keep you on track. Use your phone or a planner to set alerts for your resilience activities. Tracking milestones is another effective strategy. Celebrate small wins, like sticking to your routine for a week or noticing a positive shift in your mood. These celebrations reinforce your commitment and keep you motivated.

Flexibility and adaptation are critical to maintaining a resilience-building routine. Life is unpredictable, and your routine should adapt to different circumstances. On busy days, shorten your practices rather than skipping them altogether. If you usually meditate for ten minutes, try five minutes instead. The key is to maintain the habit, even if it's modified. Similarly, adjust your routine based on different phases of your life. During stressful periods, you might need more time for relaxation techniques. During calmer times, you could focus more on goal-setting and self-compassion practices. Being flexible ensures that your routine supports you, no matter what life throws your way.

In ending this chapter, it's essential to understand that developing a resilience-building routine is ongoing. Regular practice, maintaining motivation, and being flexible will help you build a strong foundation for emotional resilience. This routine will support you in navigating life's challenges with greater ease and confidence. Next, we will explore the importance of integrating these practices into daily life, guiding how to make them a lasting part of your well-being toolkit.

CHAPTER EIGHT

INTEGRATING SOMATIC PRACTICES INTO DAILY LIFE

One evening, while sharing dinner with my friend Howard, a widower, he sighed and confessed that eating had become a rushed, mindless activity. Between work, caring for his children, and managing household responsibilities, he barely had time to savor his meals. He felt disconnected from his body, often eating out of stress rather than hunger. Howard's story is all too familiar whether you are male or female. It's easy to fall into the habit of eating on autopilot, missing out on the nourishment and joy that mindful eating can provide. This chapter explores how integrating mindful eating into daily life can enhance somatic awareness and well-being.

MINDFUL EATING AND SOMATIC AWARENESS

Mindful eating as taught by many Eastern spiritual teachers, is the practice of being fully attentive to your food, feelings, hunger, and satiety cues. It involves eating consciously, engaging all your senses, and acknowledging responses, emotions, and physical cues like hunger or fullness. When practiced regularly, mindful eating can transform your relationship with food and your body. It encourages you to be present while eating, savoring each bite and noticing textures, flavors, and aromas. This presence allows you to tune into your body's needs, recognizing when you're starving and when you are full. By being present, you can also appreciate the effort and love that went into preparing your meal, fostering a deeper connection with your food.

The benefits of mindful eating extend beyond the dining table. It has a profound impact on digestion and emotional health. When you're mindful of what and how you eat, your body can better digest and assimilate nutrients. This mindfulness can improve digestion, reduce bloating, and increase energy levels. Emotionally, mindful eating helps you break free from stress or boredom eating. You become more aware of emotional triggers and develop healthier coping mechanisms. Instead of reaching for a snack when stressed, take a walk, practice deep breathing, or engage in a relaxing activity.

Incorporating mindfulness into meals can be straightforward. Start by setting aside time for eating, free from distractions like phones, TV, or work. Begin your meal with a few deep breaths to center yourself and bring your focus to the present moment. Pay attention to your hunger and fullness cues. Ask yourself if you're truly hungry or eating out of habit or emotion. Take small bites and chew slowly as you eat, savoring the flavors and textures. Notice the colors and aromas of your food. Engage all your senses in the eating experience.

Recognizing emotional triggers for eating is an essential aspect of mindful eating. Many of us eat not because we're hungry but because we're stressed, bored, or seeking comfort. By becoming aware of these triggers, you can make more conscious choices. For example, if you notice that you tend to snack when you're anxious, you can explore alternative ways to manage anxiety, such as practicing breathwork or taking a short walk. Understanding your body's responses to different foods is also crucial. Pay attention to how you feel after eating certain foods. Do you feel energized and satisfied or sluggish and bloated? This awareness can guide you to make healthier food choices, supporting your well-being.

A few practical strategies can help overcome challenges in mindful eating. Eating mindlessly while chatting with friends or family can be tempting in social situations. I have learned through the years to center myself before the meal and set an intention to eat mindfully. Many of us were raised in homes where a blessing was offered before starting the meal. There is definitely something to consider here even if you aren't religious. It's the pause taken in the blessing that is a reminder of all those who prepared the meal, grew the food and delivered it to your table. After the blessing, you can still enjoy the social interaction while being aware of your eating.

If distractions are an issue, you can create a calm and peaceful eating environment at home by lighting some candles and playing soft soothing music or try sitting by a window with a view. These small changes can enhance your mindfulness practice. When either my husband or I have had a particularly stressful day, instead of sitting at the breakfast table, we eat our evening meal in our newly decorated dining room. Just a change of venue can help change your mindset.

Reflection Section

Take a moment to reflect on your current eating habits. How often do you eat mindlessly, and what triggers this behavior? Write down a few observations. Then, consider one or two mindful eating practices you can incorporate into your daily routine. Consider setting aside time for meals or practicing deep breathing before eating. Notice how these changes affect your relationship with food and your overall well-being.

USING SOMATIC TECHNIQUES AT WORK

Imagine sitting at your desk, feeling the familiar tension creeping into your shoulders and neck. The workday can be a breeding ground for stress, but integrating somatic practices into your routine can make a world of difference. These techniques not only help reduce stress but also boost productivity and focus. Frequent breaks and movement are crucial. Taking short, intentional breaks throughout the day gives your body a chance to reset. A few moments of stretching or walking can release built-up tension and improve circulation. This practice makes it easier to return to your tasks with a clear mind and renewed energy.

Body awareness plays a significant role in maintaining focus. When you know your posture and how your body feels, you can adjust to stay comfortable and alert. This awareness prevents the physical discomfort that often leads to distraction and fatigue. Consider starting with simple desk stretches. Raise your arms overhead and interlace your fingers, then gently stretch to each side. Roll your shoulders forward and backward to release tension. Take a moment to check your posture—are your feet flat on the floor, and is your back supported? Small adjustments can significantly affect how you feel and perform throughout the day.

Breathing exercises offer quick stress relief and can easily be incorporated into your work routine. When you feel overwhelmed, take a few minutes to practice deep breathing. Sit comfortably, close your eyes, and take a slow, deep breath through your nose, allowing your abdomen to rise. Hold for a moment, then exhale slowly through your mouth as if you are blowing through a straw. Repeat this process a few times, focusing on the sensation of the breath entering and leaving your body. This simple exercise can calm your nervous system and help you regain focus.

Creating a somatic-friendly work environment enhances the effectiveness of these practices. Start by setting up an ergonomic workstation. Ensure your chair supports your lower back and your feet rest flat on the floor. Position your computer screen at eye level to prevent strain on your neck. Incorporate elements like plants and natural light. Plants can improve air quality and create a calming atmosphere, while natural light helps regulate your body's internal clock, boosting mood and energy levels. If natural light isn't available, consider using a daylight lamp.

Maintaining somatic practices throughout the workday requires planning and consistency. Schedule regular movement breaks. Set a timer to remind yourself to stand up, stretch, or take a short walk every hour. These breaks don't have to be lengthy—even a few minutes can rejuvenate your body and mind. Use reminders for posture checks and breathwork. Sticky notes on your monitor or phone alarms can prompt you to take a moment to adjust your posture and practice deep breathing. Over time, these small habits can become second nature, seamlessly integrating into your work routine.

Reflection Section

Take a moment to think about your current work environment. Are there areas where you could incorporate somatic practices to reduce stress and improve focus? Write down a few ideas for desk stretches, breathing exercises, and ways to create a more ergonomic and calming workspace. Consider setting up reminders to help you maintain these practices throughout the day. Notice how these changes impact your productivity and overall well-being.

INCORPORATING SOMATIC PRACTICES INTO EXERCISE

Combining somatic awareness with exercise brings a new dimension to your workouts. It's not just about moving your body but doing so with a heightened sense of awareness. This approach can improve your body alignment and movement efficiency, making each exercise more effective and enjoyable. When you tune into your body's signals, you can better understand how to move in ways that support your health and prevent injury. Imagine doing a simple squat while focusing on how your feet connect with the ground, how your knees align with your toes, and how your back maintains its natural curve. This kind of mindful movement enhances not only your physical performance but also your overall exercise experience.

One of the most natural ways to incorporate somatic awareness into physical activity is yoga and Tai Chi. Yoga, emphasizing breath and body awareness, invites you to explore each pose mindfully. As you move through a sequence, paying attention to your breath can help you notice and release areas of tension. Tai Chi, known for its slow and deliberate movements, encourages a deep connection with your body's rhythms. Each movement in Tai Chi is performed with mindful attention, promoting balance and coordination. These practices improve your physical health and foster a sense of inner calm and presence.

You can also add somatic awareness to any exercise routine with a few simple techniques. Start by paying attention to body sensations during your workouts. Whether lifting weights, running, or dancing, take moments to check in with your body. Notice how your muscles feel, how your joints move, and how your breath flows. This awareness helps you make adjustments to improve your form and prevent injury. Using breath to enhance movement and endurance is another powerful technique. For example, synchronizing your breath with your movements can make a strenuous activity like running feel more fluid and less taxing. Inhale deeply as you prepare for a movement, and exhale as you execute it. This rhythmic breathing supports your physical efforts and keeps you grounded and focused.

Recovery and self-care post-exercise are just as important as the workout itself. Somatic practices can play a crucial role in helping your body recover and maintain its health. Gentle stretching after a workout can help release any muscle tension. Focus on areas that tend to hold stress, like hamstrings, lower back, and shoulders. Self-massage techniques can further aid in releasing tight muscles and improving circulation. Spend a few minutes rolling out your muscles and applying gentle pressure to areas that feel particularly tight or sore.

Relaxation exercises are also invaluable for recovery. After an intense workout, take time to engage in activities that promote relaxation and restoration. You could do guided meditation, deep breathing exercises, or simply lie down and focus on the sensations in your body. Allow yourself to relax and let go of any remaining tension entirely. These practices help your muscles recover and support your nervous system, reducing stress and promoting overall well-being.

Incorporating these somatic practices into your exercise routine can transform your physical activities into a more mindful and holistic experience. You'll improve your physical health and cultivate a deeper connection with your body, enhancing both your workouts and overall sense of well-being. As you continue to explore and integrate these practices, you'll find that they become a natural and cherished part of your daily life.

APPLYING SOMATIC PRINCIPLES TO RELATIONSHIPS

Imagine sitting with your partner after a long day, feeling the stress of unresolved issues hanging in the air. It's easy for emotions to run high and for misunderstandings to escalate. Somatic awareness can profoundly impact your relationships by helping you recognize and regulate these emotional responses. When you're attuned to your body, you can sense the early signs of stress or agitation, such as a tightening in your chest or a clenching of your jaw. By noticing these physical cues, you can take steps to calm yourself before reacting, fostering a more thoughtful and measured response. This self-awareness helps you manage your emotions and enhances your empathy and connection with others. When you're present in your body, you're more attuned to the subtle cues in your partner's body language, allowing for deeper understanding and connection.

Practicing somatic awareness during social interactions involves a few practical strategies. Before a conversation, take a moment to ground yourself. Grounding exercises can be as simple as feeling your feet firmly planted on the floor or taking a few deep breaths to center yourself. These practices help you start the interaction from a place of calm and stability. During the conversation, use your breath to manage stress and stay present. If you notice your mind wandering or your emotions rising, take a slow, deep breath to return to the moment. This simple act can create a sense of space and clarity, allowing you to respond rather than react. Another technique is to check in with your body periodically. Notice any areas of tension and consciously relax them. This ongoing awareness helps you stay connected to your physical and emotional state, enhancing your ability to engage meaningfully with others.

Somatic practices are also incredibly effective in conflict resolution. Disagreements can quickly escalate when we're not in tune with our bodies. The Brave Thinking Institute recommends you "Notice what You're Noticing!" Recognizing the physical signs of stress, such as increased heart rate or muscle tension, allows you to intervene early. Techniques like deep breathing or progressive muscle relaxation can calm your nervous system, making it easier to approach the conflict with a clear mind. Maintaining open and empathetic communication is key. When calm and present, you can better listen actively and respond empathetically. This doesn't mean you suppress your feelings; instead, you express them in a way that fosters understanding and resolution. For instance, instead of saying, "You never listen to me," you might say, "I feel unheard when you interrupt me." This shift in language, supported by somatic awareness, creates a more constructive dialogue.

Incorporating somatic practices within family dynamics can also bring profound benefits. Family mindfulness exercises can create moments of connection and calm amidst the busyness of daily life. Simple practices like a family breathing session before dinner or a group body scan before bed can help everyone wind down and reconnect. Encouraging body awareness in children and partners is equally important. Teach your children to recognize and name their emotions and the physical sensations that accompany them. This practice helps them manage their feelings and fosters a sense of empathy and connection within the family. For example, if your child is feeling anxious, guide them to take a few deep breaths and notice how their body feels. This shared practice can become a valuable tool for navigating emotions together.

Being attuned to your body can transform your relationships in subtle yet powerful ways. It allows you to navigate interactions with greater awareness and empathy, fostering deeper connections and harmonious dynamics. Whether addressing conflicts or simply sharing a quiet moment with loved ones, somatic awareness provides a foundation for meaningful and supportive relationships. As you continue to integrate these practices into your daily life, you'll likely find your interactions more fulfilling and less stressful, enriching your overall well-being.

MAKING SOMATIC PRACTICES A LIFELONG HABIT

Imagine you've found a new hobby that brings you joy and balance. You wouldn't dabble in it once or twice and then set it aside. The same principle applies to somatic practices. Committing to these practices for the long haul offers sustained physical and emotional health benefits. It's about creating a routine that supports greater resilience and well-being over time. Your body and mind thrive on consistency. When you make somatic practices a lifelong habit, you're setting a foundation for ongoing health and emotional stability.

To maintain consistency in your somatic practices, create a flexible schedule. Life can be unpredictable, so having a routine that allows for adjustments can make it easier to stick with it. You may prefer to practice somatic exercises in the morning, but some days are busier than others. On those days, you can shift your practice to the evening. The key is to be adaptable. Setting realistic and achievable goals is also crucial. Rather than aiming for an hour-long session daily, start with 10-15 minutes. Over time, you can gradually increase the duration as it becomes a natural part of your routine. Small, consistent steps are more sustainable and manageable.

Staying motivated and engaged with your somatic practices is essential to making them a lifelong habit. Exploring new somatic exercises and techniques is one way to keep things interesting. Variety can prevent your routine from becoming monotonous. Try different forms of movement, breathing exercises, or mindfulness practices to see what resonates with you. Joining community groups or classes can also provide support and accountability. Whether it's a local yoga class or an online TranscenDANCE movement class, these communities offer encouragement and the opportunity to share experiences.

Ongoing learning and adaptation are vital for evolving your somatic practice. Reading books and attending workshops on somatic therapy can deepen your understanding and introduce you to new concepts and techniques. Look for resources that offer practical insights and exercises to incorporate into your routine. Adapting your practices to meet changing needs and life circumstances is equally important. As you age, your body and mind will go through different phases. What worked for you a few years ago might need adjustments to fit your current state. Listen to your body and be willing to modify your practices as needed. This flexibility ensures that your somatic practices continue to support your well-being effectively.

Incorporating somatic practices into your daily life doesn't have to be a daunting task. It's about finding what works best for you and making it a natural part of your routine. Think of it as a form of self-care that nourishes your body and mind. Each practice, whether a brief moment of mindful breathing or a more extended movement session, contributes to your overall well-being. The benefits of making somatic practices a lifelong habit extend beyond immediate relief. Over time, you'll notice greater emotional resilience, improved physical health, and a deeper connection with yourself. It's a commitment to nurturing your well-being, one mindful step at a time.

This chapter explored how to integrate somatic practices into daily life, from mindful eating to enhancing relationships. By making these practices a lifelong habit, you're setting the stage for sustained well-being. Next, we'll delve into how to track your progress and stay motivated, ensuring that you continue to reap the benefits of your somatic practices.

CHAPTER NINE

BUILDING A SUPPORTIVE COMMUNITY

I was teaching an energy healing class a few years ago when a woman named Sallie was in the class. She had been through a lot—divorce, the loss of a close friend, and the stress of balancing work and family. Despite her challenges, Sallie radiated a sense of peace and resilience. Curious, I asked her about her secret. She smiled and said, "I found my tribe." Sallie explained that joining a local support group had transformed her life. The community provided her with emotional support, shared experiences, and a sense of belonging that she had been missing. Sallie's story highlights a supportive community's profound impact on our healing process.

THE IMPORTANCE OF COMMUNITY IN HEALING

Having a supportive community is crucial for emotional and physical healing. When you share your experiences with others who understand what you're going through, you receive emotional support and validation that can be incredibly healing. It's comforting to know that you're not alone in your struggles and that others have faced similar challenges. This sense of shared experience fosters mutual understanding and empathy, creating a safe space where you can be open and vulnerable. Feeling seen and heard makes it easier to process and release the emotions tied to your experiences.

The benefits of a supportive network extend beyond emotional support. Being part of a healing community can increase your motivation and accountability. Committing to a group makes you more likely to stay consistent with your healing practices. Group members often encourage each other to keep going, celebrate each other's progress, and provide gentle reminders to stay on track. This sense of accountability can be a powerful motivator, helping you stay committed to your healing journey. Additionally, a supportive community can reduce feelings of isolation and loneliness. Knowing you have a network of people who care about your well-being can provide immense comfort and reassurance, especially during challenging times.

The concept of collective healing is based on the idea that healing within a community can enhance individual progress. When people come together with a shared intention to heal, the collective energy amplifies the healing process. In his book Think and Grow Rich, Napoleon Hill wrote about this nearly a hundred years ago. He called these groups "Masterminds." Andrew Carnegie asked Hill to interview the 500 wealthiest people in the United States to find out why and how they became successful. Hill discovered that practically all of them belonged to mastermind groups where two or more people coordinate in a spirit of harmony and work toward a definite objective. This phenomenon is often referred to as the power of group energy. Group energy can create a supportive and nurturing environment that accelerates individual healing. For example, group meditation or breathwork sessions can generate a palpable sense of calm and connection, making it easier for each participant to relax and release tension. Collective intention can also be compelling, where all members focus on a common goal or outcome. Whether it's setting a group intention for peace, healing, or transformation, the group's combined energy can manifest significant positive changes.

There are many examples of successful collective healing efforts. One notable example is the community of An Infinite Mind, founded by Jaime Pollack. This organization provides support for individuals with dissociative identity disorder (DID) and has created a safe space for connection and healing. Members of this community report feeling a profound sense of belonging and support, which has been instrumental in their healing process. Another example is the Powerhouse Women community, which offers a space for connection and empowerment. Members of this group have found solace and strength in the community's shared experiences and mutual support.

A few years back, I discovered a supportive group created by the new thought leader, Mary Morrissey, at the Brave Thinking Institute. I became a certified transformational coach with them and have remained in one or more of their programs for many years. During COVID, we shifted to weekly Zoom calls when no one could meet in person. Since then, technology has expanded to help us stay connected even though we cannot or choose not to travel. The programs at the Brave Thinking Institute are rewarding and enriching gatherings that support individuals on their quests to grow and expand their horizons.

Reflection Section

Take a moment to reflect on your current support network. Do you have a group of people who provide emotional support and validation? If not, consider seeking out a community where you can share your experiences and receive the support you need. Write down the qualities you would like in a supportive community and consider where you might find such a group.

Real-life testimonials further illustrate the power of community in healing. One woman, Emily, shared how she found comfort in a local support group after her husband passed away. The group provided her with a safe space to express her grief and receive support from others who had experienced similar losses. Through the group, Emily felt understood and validated, which helped her navigate her grief and begin to heal. Another reader, Ashley, experienced accelerated healing through community involvement. She joined a somatic therapy group where members practiced mindfulness and shared their progress. The group's collective energy and mutual support helped Ashley stay motivated and committed to her healing practices, significantly improving her emotional well-being.

In summary, a supportive community is vital to the healing process. Emotional support and validation, shared experiences, and mutual understanding create a safe space for healing. The benefits of a supportive network include increased motivation, accountability, and reduced feelings of isolation. Collective healing within a community can amplify individual progress through the power of group energy and collective intention. Real-life examples and testimonials demonstrate the transformative impact of community support on emotional and physical healing.

FINDING OR CREATING A LOCAL SUPPORT GROUP

Finding a local support group can be a rewarding experience. It starts with a bit of research and a willingness to explore your community. Begin by checking community centers and local wellness clinics. These places often host various support groups and may have information on Somatic Therapy or holistic healing groups. Don't hesitate to ask the staff for recommendations; they are usually well-informed about local resources.

Social media and online directories are also valuable tools. Websites like Meetup.com can help you locate somatic therapy groups in your area. Enter your location and search for keywords like "Somatic Therapy," "holistic healing," or "mindfulness." You might be surprised at how many groups are available. Facebook is another excellent platform. Many communities have private groups dedicated to specific interests, including somatic practices. Joining these groups can provide immediate access to local events and meetups.

Being part of a face-to-face community offers numerous benefits. One of the most significant advantages is the immediate feedback and personal interaction you receive. In-person meetings allow you to connect deeper, building trust and forming meaningful relationships. This kind of connection fosters a sense of belonging and makes sharing personal experiences and challenges easier. Face-to-face interactions also allow observing body language and other non-verbal cues, enhancing understanding and empathy among group members.

If you are still looking for suitable groups in your area, consider creating your own. It might seem daunting initially, but you can establish a supportive and nurturing community with a few steps. Start by finding a suitable meeting space. This could be a room at a community center, a local library, or a cozy cafe. Ensure the space is comfortable and private enough for open discussions. Once you have a location, set clear group goals and guidelines. Define the purpose of the group and what you hope to achieve. Establishing ground rules for respectful communication and confidentiality will create a safe environment for all members.

Collaboration and resource sharing are key components of a successful support group. Encourage members to share their knowledge and resources. You could consider organizing group activities and workshops where members can learn new techniques and practices. For instance, one meeting could focus on guided meditation, while another might involve a hands-on aromatherapy session. Exchanging books, articles, and other materials can enrich the group's collective knowledge. Create a lending library where members can borrow and share resources.

Resource List

- Community Centers and Local Wellness Clinics: Check bulletin boards and ask staff for information on existing support groups.
- Meetup.com: Search for local somatic therapy or holistic healing groups.
- Facebook: Join private groups dedicated to somatic practices and local events.
- Libraries and Cafes: Consider these spaces for hosting your support group meetings.

By following these steps, you can find or create a local support group that provides the emotional and practical support you need. Building a community takes effort, but the benefits of having a network of like-minded individuals can be life-changing.

ONLINE COMMUNITIES AND RESOURCES

Online communities can be a lifeline for those seeking support, especially when in-person groups aren't an option. One of the biggest advantages is accessibility. You can connect with like-minded individuals from the comfort of your home without the need to travel or adjust your schedule drastically. This convenience means that no matter where you live, you can find a community that understands and supports you. Additionally, online platforms are available 24/7, providing support whenever you need it most, whether it's early in the morning or late at night.

Another benefit of online communities is their diverse perspectives and experiences. When you join an online group, you're not limited to the views and experiences of those in your immediate geographic area. Instead, you gain access to a global network of people who bring varied insights and solutions to the table. This diversity can be incredibly enriching, broadening your understanding and introducing you to new approaches and ideas. For example, you might learn about different somatic therapy techniques that are only sometimes practiced in your area or gain inspiration from someone who has overcome similar challenges.

Several reputable online platforms and forums can provide valuable support for somatic therapy. Dedicated Facebook groups are an excellent starting point. These groups often have thousands of members and are moderated to ensure a safe and supportive environment. You can find groups explicitly focused on somatic therapy, mindfulness, and holistic healing. Online forums and discussion boards, such as those found on Reddit and HealthUnlocked, offer another avenue for connection. These platforms allow for in-depth discussions, sharing of resources, and building long-term relationships with other members.

When engaging in online communities, it's crucial to interact respectfully and constructively. Practicing active listening and empathy can make a significant difference in the quality of your interactions. Active listening involves genuinely hearing what others say without immediately jumping in with your thoughts or advice. It means acknowledging their feelings and experiences, which fosters a supportive atmosphere. Avoiding judgment and offering supportive comments are also essential. Everyone's journey is unique; what works for one person might not work for another. By maintaining a non-judgmental attitude and focusing on encouragement, you contribute to a positive and uplifting community.

Maximizing your involvement in online groups requires a bit of strategy. Participating in regular discussions and events is a good start. Many online communities host virtual events, such as webinars, summits, guided meditations, or Q&A sessions with experts. These events provide valuable learning opportunities and help you feel more connected to the group. Reaching out to connect with other members individually can also enhance your experience. Building one-on-one relationships within the group can provide additional support and deepen your sense of belonging. Don't hesitate to send a private message to someone whose story resonates with you or to ask for advice on a specific issue.

Resource List

- Facebook Groups: Search for groups like "Somatic Therapy Support" or "Mindfulness and Healing."
- Reddit: Subreddits such as r/SomaticTherapy and r/Mindfulness offer supportive communities.
- HealthUnlocked: Join forums focused on holistic health and somatic practices.
- Meetup.com: Look for virtual somatic therapy meetups and online groups.

Incorporating these online communities into your support network can give you the necessary resources and connections. Whether looking for advice, inspiration, or just a listening ear, the online world offers many opportunities to enrich your healing journey.

SHARING YOUR SOMATIC JOURNEY WITH OTHERS

Sharing your personal experiences can be incredibly healing, not just for you but for those who hear your story. Verbalizing your experiences can provide therapeutic benefits, helping you process and make sense of your emotions. When you share your journey, you create a sense of shared humanity. Others see themselves in your story, which can foster connection and inspire them to share their experiences. It's a powerful form of mutual healing that can break down feelings of isolation and build a community of understanding and support.

When sharing your story, it's important to do so in a safe and comfortable way. Setting boundaries is crucial. Decide what you are comfortable sharing and what you'd prefer to keep private. Practicing vulnerability while maintaining self-protection means being honest, open, and mindful of your emotional limits. It's okay to share selectively and to protect parts of your story that feel too raw or personal. This balance allows you to connect with others without feeling overexposed or vulnerable to judgment.

There are various platforms where you can share your somatic journey. Writing blog posts or articles is a wonderful way to reach a broad audience. You can narrate your experiences, share insights, and advise others on a similar path. Blogs and articles allow you to control the narrative and share at your own pace. Speaking at support group meetings or community events is another effective way to share your story. These settings provide a more intimate environment where you can engage directly with your audience, answer questions, and offer real-time support.

Creative expression offers another outlet for sharing your journey. Art, music, and poetry can convey emotions and experiences in ways that words alone might not capture. Creating visual art pieces depicting your healing process can be therapeutic and inspiring for others. Whether painting, drawing or even crafting, these visual representations can be powerful symbols of your growth and resilience. Composing music or poetry allows you to express your experiences through sound and rhythm. These forms of expression can touch people deeply emotionally, creating a shared space for healing and connection.

Reflection Section

Consider how you might share your story. What platform feels most comfortable for you? Reflect on the parts of your journey you're ready to share and think about the impact your story might have on others. Write down your thoughts and any creative ideas that come to mind.

FOSTERING CONNECTION AND EMPATHY IN YOUR COMMUNITY

Empathy is the cornerstone of any thriving community. It's the glue that binds us together, fostering deeper connections and understanding. When you practice empathy, you actively listen to others, validating their experiences and emotions. This act of listening creates a non-judgmental and supportive environment where everyone feels safe to share their thoughts and feelings. Imagine sitting in a circle, each person taking turns to speak while the rest listen attentively, nodding in understanding. This simple act of being heard can be profoundly healing, making each member feel valued and respected. I have personally belonged to women's circles for many decades and can attest to the power of women helping women. One such circle started as a drumming circle where we would share our lives and receive rich support and encouragement to move forward with our dreams.

To cultivate empathy within your community, start with reflective listening. Reflective listening involves hearing the words spoken and understanding the emotions behind them. When someone shares their story, reflect on what you've listened to, acknowledging their feelings. For example, if a member talks about feeling overwhelmed, you might respond, "It sounds like you've been carrying a heavy load lately, and it's been really tough." This validation helps individuals feel understood and supported. Engaging in empathy-building exercises can also be beneficial. Activities like role-playing or sharing personal experiences in pairs can enhance your ability to empathize with others. These exercises help you step into someone else's shoes, broadening your perspective and deepening your compassion.

Shared activities are another effective way to foster connections within your community. Group meditation or mindfulness sessions can create a sense of unity and collective calm. Imagine everyone sitting in a circle, eyes closed, breathing in unison. The group's collective energy can amplify the benefits of meditation, helping each member feel more centered and connected. Collaborative art projects or workshops offer another avenue for building bonds. Whether painting a mural together or participating in a pottery class, these activities provide a creative outlet and a shared goal, strengthening the sense of community. Working on a project together allows for natural conversations and camaraderie, making it easier to form lasting connections.

Maintaining and strengthening community connections requires ongoing engagement. Regularly scheduled group meetings and check-ins are crucial. These meetings don't have to be formal or lengthy; even a casual coffee meet-up can allow members to reconnect and support each other. Consistency is key. Knowing a regular meeting time and place can provide stability and continuity, fostering a deeper sense of belonging. Organizing community events and gatherings can also keep the momentum going. Consider hosting themed events like a mindfulness retreat, a wellness workshop, or a celebratory potluck. These gatherings offer a chance for members to interact in different settings, deepening their relationships and enhancing the overall sense of community.

Reflection Section

Take a moment to think about how you can foster empathy and connection within your community. What activities or practices could you introduce to enhance understanding and support? Write down any ideas that come to mind and consider discussing them at your next group meeting.

Empathy and connection are the lifeblood of any supportive community. By practicing active listening, engaging in empathy-building activities, and organizing shared experiences, you can create a nurturing environment where everyone feels valued and understood. Regular engagement through meetings and events will keep these connections strong, ensuring that your community remains a source of strength and healing for all its members.

In the next chapter, we'll explore how to track your progress and stay motivated on your healing path. Tracking progress helps you see how far you've come and keeps you focused and inspired to continue your journey toward well-being.

CHAPTER TEN

TRACKING PROGRESS AND STAYING MOTIVATED

Not long ago, I started working with a new client, Pat. Since she lived in another state, our weekly calls were by Zoom. Pat wanted to work with me because she had trouble staying motivated in her desire to move forward in her life. She was married to her life partner who was quite content with his life and had no intention of changing anything. Conversely, Pat was a "bored housewife" who knew there was more to life to explore. Having a coach, she thought, would help keep her motivated to make changes. She recognized that she wasn't thriving but lacked internal motivation until then. She was hoping I could offer her ways to change her way of thinking and be able to self-motivate.

THE IMPORTANCE OF TRACKING YOUR PROGRESS

Imagine standing in your garden, nurturing a variety of plants. You water them, give them sunlight, and occasionally, you might even talk to them. Over time, you notice some plants thriving while others struggle. You note what works and what doesn't, adjusting your care routine to help every plant flourish. This careful observation and adjustment are akin to tracking your progress in Somatic Therapy. Monitoring your journey is like tending to that garden, ensuring that every part of your well-being receives the attention it needs to grow strong and healthy.

One of the ways I helped my new client Pat was by showing her how to track her progress giving her a clear picture of where she started, where she is now, and where she wanted to go. This daily visual not only showed her progress, but helped her see that yes, she can change within her circumstances.

Tracking your progress brings awareness to improvements and setbacks, allowing you to celebrate successes and promptly address challenges. For instance, you might notice that your anxiety levels have decreased after a month of practicing mindful breathing. On the flip side, you might find that specific stressors still trigger physical discomfort. This awareness is crucial for making informed decisions about your healing practices, ensuring that you stay on the right path.

One of the most effective ways to track your progress is through journaling. Daily journaling your experiences, emotions, and physical sensations can provide valuable insights. Each entry is a snapshot of your day, capturing small victories and lingering challenges. Over time, these snapshots create a comprehensive picture of your progress. You might write about a particularly stressful day and how you used grounding techniques to manage your anxiety. Later, you can look back and see how your responses have evolved, reinforcing the effectiveness of your practices.

Digital apps designed for progress tracking can also be invaluable tools. Apps like Daylio, recommended by Healthline, offer mood tracking, goal setting, and daily reflections. You can identify patterns and triggers by inputting your mood and activities, helping you understand what contributes to your well-being. Another helpful app, MindShift CBT, provides tools for coping with anxiety through cognitive-behavioral techniques. These apps make it easy to document your journey, providing visual representations of your progress that can be incredibly motivating.

Regular reflection is another vital component of tracking your progress. Setting aside weekly time to review your experiences can deepen your understanding and commitment to your healing journey. During these reflection sessions, ask yourself questions like, "What went well this week?" and "What challenges did I face?" Reflecting on these questions helps you identify patterns and make necessary adjustments. For instance, you might feel more balanced when incorporating breathwork into your morning routine. This insight can motivate you to make breathwork a regular part of your day.

Consider the case of Sara, a 58-year-old woman who began her somatic therapy journey six months ago. Sara used a progress journal to document her daily practices and reflections. She noted her physical sensations, emotional states, and the techniques she used to manage them. Over time, Sara noticed significant improvements in her emotional resilience and a decrease in chronic pain. Her journal entries provided tangible evidence of her progress, reinforcing her commitment to Somatic Therapy. Sara's story highlights the power of tracking progress and the motivation it can provide.

Another example is Margaret, who found that using a mobile app to track her progress made a significant difference. Margaret used the app to record her daily mood, activities, and physical sensations. The app provided visual charts that showed her progress over time—the gradual improvement in her mood and reduced physical discomfort motivated Margaret to continue her practices. The app also allowed her to set reminders for her daily somatic exercises, ensuring she stayed consistent. Margaret's success story illustrates how digital tools can enhance your tracking efforts and motivate you.

Reflection Section

Take a moment to reflect on your current approach to tracking your progress. Do you keep a journal, use a digital app, or rely on memory? Consider incorporating a more structured method to monitor your journey. Write down one or two new strategies you can implement to track your progress more effectively. Consider setting a specific time each week for reflection and review. How might these changes enhance your understanding and commitment to somatic therapy practices?

Incorporating these tracking methods into your routine can provide a clearer perspective on your progress. Whether through journaling, digital apps, or regular reflection, tracking your journey allows you to celebrate your successes and address challenges more clearly. It's a powerful way to stay motivated, ensuring you continue to nurture your well-being and achieve the balance you seek.

USING WORKSHEETS AND TOOLS FOR SELF-ASSESSMENT

Self-assessment in somatic therapy is like looking into a mirror that reflects your inner and outer self. It's a valuable tool for personal growth and understanding. Regular self-assessment helps you identify your strengths and areas where you need extra care or attention. It's about checking in with yourself to gauge your emotional and physical states, ensuring that you're not just moving through life on autopilot. Think of it as an ongoing dialogue with yourself, where you take the time to listen to and interpret the signals your body and mind are sending. This practice fosters self-awareness and empowers you to make informed decisions about your well-being.

Using specific worksheets can be incredibly helpful in facilitating this process. A daily symptom tracker, for instance, allows you to note any physical sensations, emotional states, and stressors you experience each day. This worksheet can include sections for tracking pain levels, mood fluctuations, energy levels, and any somatic practices you engage in. By consistently filling out this tracker, you can identify patterns and correlations between your activities and how you feel. For example, you might notice that your anxiety levels are lower when you practice breathwork. This insight can guide you in prioritizing activities that enhance your well-being.

Another helpful tool is a weekly goal-setting and reflection sheet. This worksheet encourages you to set specific, achievable goals at the beginning of each week and reflect on your progress at the end. Setting goals helps you stay focused and motivated, while the reflection section allows you to evaluate what worked well and what didn't. For instance, you might set a goal to incorporate a new somatic exercise into your routine. At the end of the week, you can reflect on how this practice affected your physical and emotional state. Did it bring relief? Was it challenging to maintain? This reflection helps you fine-tune your approach and stay on track.

Digital tools can also simplify and enhance your self-assessment process. Numerous apps are available that can help you track your mood, symptoms, and goals. Apps like Daylio and Moodfit are designed to make tracking easy and accessible. They offer features like mood journaling, symptom tracking, and goal setting, all in one place. Using these apps, you can quickly log your daily experiences and review your progress. These apps' visual data can be particularly motivating, allowing you to see tangible improvements and areas needing attention.

Online platforms can also be beneficial for setting and reviewing goals. Websites like Trello or Notion offer customizable templates for goal setting, progress tracking, and reflection. These platforms provide a flexible and organized way to manage your self-assessment activities. For example, you can create a Trello board with columns for daily symptom tracking, weekly goals, and reflection. Each card can represent a day or a week, making it easy to review your progress and adjust as needed.

Making self-assessment a consistent practice requires some practical strategies. Setting reminders can be a simple yet effective way to ensure you regularly check in with yourself. You can set daily or weekly reminders on your phone or calendar to prompt you to fill out your worksheets or use digital tools. These reminders help you develop a routine, making self-assessment a natural part of your day.

Combining self-assessment with other somatic practices can also enhance its effectiveness. For instance, you can integrate your self-assessment activities into your mindfulness or meditation sessions. After a mindfulness exercise, take a few minutes to reflect on how you feel and note any observations in your journal or app. This integration ensures that you practice somatic techniques and actively monitor their impact on your well-being.

Imagine using a daily symptom tracker to log your experiences. You start each morning by noting your baseline mood and any physical sensations. Throughout the day, you jot down any significant changes or stressors. In the evening, you review your entries, reflecting on how the day went and what practices helped. This daily tracking keeps you in tune with your body and mind, making it easier to identify what supports your well-being.

Similarly, a weekly goal-setting and reflection sheet can provide structure and motivation. At the start of each week, you set clear, achievable goals, such as practicing a new somatic exercise or incorporating more mindfulness into your routine. At the end of the week, you reflect on your progress, noting any challenges and successes. This reflection helps you adjust your approach and stay focused on your well-being.

Digital tools and online platforms can further streamline this process. Apps like Daylio allow you to quickly log your mood and activities, providing visual data highlighting trends and patterns. Online platforms like Trello or Notion offer customizable templates for tracking your goals and progress. These tools make it easy to stay organized and motivated, ensuring self-assessment becomes a routine.

Incorporating these self-assessment practices into your daily life can significantly enhance your understanding of your emotional and physical states. Regularly checking in with yourself makes you more attuned to your needs and allows you to make informed decisions about your somatic therapy practices. This ongoing dialogue with yourself fosters self-awareness, empowering you to take control of your well-being and create a balanced, fulfilling life.

STAYING MOTIVATED AND OVERCOMING OBSTACLES

Motivation can be a tricky thing. It's easy to start strong but maintaining that momentum over the long haul is another story. One common challenge you may face is the need for immediate results. You've committed to somatic therapy, you're doing the exercises, and yet, it feels like nothing is changing. This can be incredibly frustrating. It's akin to planting a seed and expecting a flower the next day. Healing, much like gardening, takes time. The small, incremental changes can quickly go unnoticed, making you feel like your efforts are in vain.

External stressors and life changes also play a significant role in disrupting your progress. Life is full of unexpected events—family emergencies, work deadlines, or a hectic week. These stressors can throw you off track, making it difficult to maintain your routine. It's easy to feel overwhelmed and think, "I'll get back to it when things calm down." But the truth is, life rarely slows down. Despite the chaos, finding a way to integrate your practices into your daily life is crucial for long-term success.

So, how do you stay motivated amidst these challenges? One effective strategy is setting realistic and achievable milestones. You want to break down your larger goals into smaller, manageable steps. For instance, instead of aiming to practice somatic techniques for an hour every day, start with just ten minutes. Once that becomes a habit, gradually increase the time. Achieving these smaller milestones provides a sense of accomplishment and motivates you to continue. It's like climbing a mountain one step at a time—each step brings you closer to the summit.

Celebrating small victories can also keep your spirits high. Don't wait until you've achieved your ultimate goal to celebrate. Acknowledge and reward yourself for the little wins along the way. Did you manage to practice mindful breathing every day this week? Treat yourself to a relaxing bath or a favorite activity. These small celebrations reinforce your progress and make the journey more enjoyable.

Support networks are invaluable for sustaining motivation. Regular check-ins with support group members can provide encouragement and accountability. Knowing that others are on a similar path and facing similar challenges can be incredibly comforting. Share your progress and setbacks with a trusted friend or therapist. Their feedback can offer new perspectives and keep you motivated. Sometimes, talking about your experiences reignites your enthusiasm and reminds you why you started in the first place.

Overcoming obstacles often requires practical, actionable tips. Time management is a common barrier. Creating a routine that incorporates your somatic practices can make a big difference. Set specific times for your exercises and stick to them like any other important appointment. Use reminders and alarms if needed. Consistency is key and having a set routine helps make your practices a regular part of your day.

Dealing with setbacks is another hurdle. It's easy to get discouraged when things don't go as planned. Maybe you missed a few days of practice, or you're not seeing the progress you hoped for. It's essential to maintain a positive mindset during these times. Remind yourself that setbacks are a natural part of any healing process. Instead of viewing them as failures, see them as opportunities to learn and grow. Failures are only feedback telling you that you have slipped off the path. Reflect on what caused the setback and how you can address it moving forward. This proactive approach keeps you focused on your long-term goals and helps you bounce back more quickly.

Consider the story of Martha, a 60-year-old woman who struggled with maintaining her somatic practices amidst a busy life. Martha found that setting realistic milestones, like practicing mindful movement for ten minutes each morning, helped her stay committed. She also celebrated her progress by treating herself to a favorite book or a day out with friends. Regular check-ins with her support group provided the encouragement and accountability Martha needed. She reflected on what went wrong when she faced setbacks and adjusted her routine accordingly. These strategies helped Martha stay motivated and overcome obstacles, significantly improving her well-being.

Incorporating these strategies into your routine can help you stay motivated and navigate the challenges of Somatic Therapy. Remember, it's about progress, not perfection. Celebrate small victories, lean on your support network, and keep a positive mindset. Over time, these practices will become second nature, and you'll find it easier to stay committed to your healing journey.

Integrating these practices into your daily life can enhance your overall well-being and create a solid foundation for healing. Next, we'll explore the importance of building a supportive community and how it can further enhance your healing journey.

KEEPING THE JOURNEY ALIVE

☆☆☆☆☆

Now that you have everything you need to find more mindfulness, stress relief, and emotional balance, it's time to share your experience with others. By leaving your honest opinion of Somatic Therapy Simplified on Amazon, you'll help other readers, especially women over 50, discover the tools and techniques to bring them the same well-being.

Your review helps others find the information they're looking for and keeps the spirit of somatic therapy alive—spreading the benefits of healing and self-care to even more people.

Thank you for your support. Somatic Therapy Simplified continues to thrive when we share our knowledge with others—and you're helping me do just that.

Scan the QR code to leave your review on Amazon.

IN CONCLUSION

As we end our journey together, I want to reflect on the vision and purpose that brought us here. This book began with my research into what people were struggling with to transform their lives at times of transition. It was crafted with a heartfelt intention to support you in finding holistic healing, achieving emotional balance, and experiencing the profound benefits of Somatic Therapy. My goal has always been to provide practical, easy-to-follow guidance that can make a real difference in your life, no matter what your age.

Throughout this book, we've explored various facets of somatic therapy, from understanding its core principles to integrating it into daily life. We've delved into the power of body awareness, the importance of breath work, and therapeutic movement's healing potential. We've discussed how to release stored trauma and manage stress and anxiety, all while building emotional resilience and fostering self-care routines.

We started by understanding Somatic Therapy and how it connects the mind and body to promote healing. We learned about its historical roots and the science behind the mind-body connection. We then moved on to practical steps, like preparing your mind and body for healing, setting intentions, and creating a safe space for practice. We've walked through specific techniques and exercises to enhance body awareness, manage stress, and release trauma. Each chapter was designed to build on the previous one, creating a comprehensive approach to holistic healing.

One of the key takeaways from our journey is the importance of body awareness. Being in tune with your physical sensations can provide valuable insights into your emotional health. Simple exercises like mindful breathing, body scanning, and gentle stretching can significantly affect your feelings. Incorporating these practices into your daily routine can enhance your overall well-being and create a solid foundation for healing.

Another important lesson is the power of breathwork and therapeutic movement like TranscenDANCE. These practices help release stored trauma and manage everyday stress and anxiety. Regular breathwork can calm your nervous system and promote relaxation, while therapeutic movement can release muscle tension and improve emotional balance.

We've also emphasized the significance of self-care and building a supportive community. Self-care is not a luxury; it's a necessity. You can build emotional resilience and prevent burnout by prioritizing your well-being and incorporating self-care practices into your routine. Finding or creating a supportive community can provide the emotional support and validation you need on your healing journey. Sharing your experiences and connecting with others can amplify your progress and make the journey more enjoyable.

Now, as you move forward, I encourage you to take action. Start by integrating the practices and techniques we've discussed into your daily life. Set aside time daily for body awareness exercises, breathwork, and self-care. Keep a journal to track your progress and reflect on your experiences. Reach out to others and build a supportive network that can provide encouragement and accountability.

Remember, healing is a journey, not a destination. It's okay to have setbacks and challenges along the way. What matters is your commitment to yourself and your well-being. Celebrate your small victories and be gentle with yourself during difficult times. Your progress, no matter how small, is a step towards a healthier, more balanced life.

In closing, I want to leave you with a message of encouragement. You have the power within you to heal and transform your life. By embracing Somatic Therapy and the holistic practices we've discussed, you can achieve emotional balance, reduce stress, and enhance your overall well-being. Believe in yourself and your ability to make positive changes. You are stronger and more resilient than you realize.

Thank you for allowing me to be a part of your journey. This book has provided the tools and inspiration to embark on your path to holistic healing. Remember, you are not alone. Reach out, connect, and continue to grow. Your journey is just beginning, and I am confident you have the strength and wisdom to navigate it with grace and resilience.

Here's to your health, happiness, and holistic well-being.

REFERENCES

Braden, G. (2014). Resilience from the Heart: The Power to Thrive in Life's Extremes. Hay House, Inc.

BrainTap. App store.

Brave Thinking Institute. (n.d.). What Is Trancendance™? Brave Thinking Institute. https://www.bravethinkinginstitute.com/evg/health-wellbeing/resources/ws/transcendance-masterclass/register/st/

Brennan, B. (1988). Hands of Light, A Guide to Healing Through the Human Energy Field. Bantum Book.

Brightside Counseling. (n.d.). Morning routines reduce stress and increase happiness. https://brightsidecounseling.com/morning-routines-your-key-to-life-satisfaction-and-stress-reduction/

Carepatron. (n.d.). Emotional release massage techniques. https://www.carepatron.com/guides/emotional-release-massage-techniques

Charlie Health. (n.d.). How somatic breathwork can help you chill out. https://www.charliehealth.com/post/somatic-breathwork#:.

Cobb Collaborative. (n.d.). Journaling as a recovery and resilience-building tool. https://www.cobbcollaborative.org/journaling-as-a-recovery-and-resilience-building-tool

Dispenza, J. (2007). Evolve your Brain, The Science of Changing your Mind. Health Communications, Inc.

Dispenza, J. (2014) You are the Placebo, Making your Mind Matter. Hay House, Inc.

Eden, D. (1998). Energy Medicine, Balance your Body's Energies for Optimum Health, Joy, and Vitality. Jermy P. Tarcher/Putnam.

Gale, J. (n.d.). How to create a sacred space for meditation. https://www.jodiegale.com/how-to-create-a-sacred-space/

Goddard, N. (1952). The Power of Awareness. Jeremy P. Tarcher/Penguin Publishers.

Healing Touch Program. https://discover.healingtouchprogram.com

Healthline. (n.d.). Body awareness: How to deepen your connection with yourself. https://www.healthline.com/health/mind-body/body-awareness

Healthline. (n.d.). Cognitive restructuring: Techniques and examples. https://www.healthline.com/health/cognitive-restructuring

Healthline. (n.d.). The best mental health apps to use in 2024. https://www.healthline.com/health/mental-health/mental-health-apps

Headspace. (n.d.). Body scan meditation to reduce stress. https://www.headspace.com/meditation/body-scan

Hello, I'm 50ish. (n.d.). The ultimate self-care guide for women over 50. https://helloim50ish.com/the-ultimate-self-care-guide-for-women-over-50/

Hill, N. (2005). Think and grow rich. (Originally published in 1937). Jeremy P. Tarcher/Penguin.

Hopkins Medicine. (n.d.). Somatic self-care. https://www.hopkinsmedicine.org/office-of-well-being/connection-support/somatic-self-care

Hover-Kramer, D. (1996). Healing Touch, A Resource for Health Care Professionals. Delmar Publishers.

Innercise™, App store.

Kirstein, M. (n.d.). 12 effective somatic therapy exercises for holistic healing. https://www.monakirstein.com/somatic-therapy-exercises/

Levine, P. A. (n.d.). Peter A. Levine, PhD — Ergos Institute, Inc™. https://www.somaticexperiencing.com/about-peter

Mayoclinic.org. (n.d.). Chronic stress puts your health at risk. https://www.mayoclinic.org/healthy-lifestyle/stress-management/in-depth/stress/art-20046037

Mayoclinic.org. (n.d.). Resilience: Build skills to endure hardship. https://www.mayoclinic.org/tests-procedures/resilience-training/in-depth/resilience/art-20046311#:.

Mayoclinic.org. (n.d.). Support groups: Make connections, get help. https://www.mayoclinic.org/healthy-lifestyle/stress-management/in-depth/support-groups/art-20044655#:

Medium. (n.d.). Best somatic psychotherapy tools to help heal trauma. https://medium.com/change-becomes-you/best-somatic-psychotherapy-tools-to-help-heal-trauma-4bcc3e428c88

Meridian University. (n.d.). Somatic psychology: Meaning and origins. https://meridianuniversity.edu/content/somatic-psychology-meaning-and-origins

Mindful.org. (n.d.). 6 ways to practice mindful eating. https://www.mindful.org/6-ways-practice-mindful-eating/

NCBI. (n.d.). Body awareness: A phenomenological inquiry into the lived experience of the body. https://www.ncbi.nlm.nih.gov/pmc/articles/PMC3096919/

NCBI. (n.d.). Monitoring treatment progress and providing feedback is critical for psychotherapy outcomes. https://www.ncbi.nlm.nih.gov/pmc/articles/PMC5495625/

NCBI. (n.d.). Somatic experiencing – effectiveness and key factors of a somatic therapy. https://www.ncbi.nlm.nih.gov/pmc/articles/PMC8276649/

NCBI. (n.d.). The polyvagal theory: New insights into adaptive reactions. https://www.ncbi.nlm.nih.gov/pmc/articles/PMC3108032/

NCBI. (n.d.). The benefits of self-compassion in mental health. https://www.ncbi.nlm.nih.gov/pmc/articles/PMC9482966/

Positive Psychology. (n.d.). How to use mindfulness therapy for anxiety: 15 exercises. https://positivepsychology.com/mindfulness-for-anxiety/

PsychCentral. (n.d.). The relationship between mindfulness and resilience. https://psychcentral.com/lib/mindfulness-the-art-of-cultivating-resilience

Psychology Today. (2022, March). Breath and trauma-healing exercises. https://www.psychologytoday.com/us/blog/the-addiction-connection/202203/breath-and-trauma-healing-exercises#:.

Psychology Today. (2022, April). The healing power of community and connection. https://www.psychologytoday.com/us/blog/keeping-it-real-and-resilient/202204/the-healing-power-of-community-and-connection

Salamon, M. (2023, July 7). What is somatic therapy? Harvard Health Publishing. https://www.health.harvard.edu/blog/what-is-somatic-therapy-202307072951

Somatic Movement Center. (n.d.). Combining your clinical somatics and yoga practices. https://somaticmovementcenter.com/somatics-yoga/#:

Two Chairs. (n.d.). Building your stress management toolkit. https://www.twochairs.com/blog/building-your-stress-management-toolkit

Van der Kolk, B. (n.d.). The body keeps the score. https://www.besselvanderkolk.com/resources/the-body-keeps-the-score

Van der Kolk, B. (2014). The Body Keeps the Score. Penguin Books.

Made in the USA
Middletown, DE
04 December 2024